Extreme Nature

Extreme

Nature

Mark Carwardine

with Rosamund Kidman Cox

Collins

HarperCollins Publishers Ltd.
77-85 Fulham Palace Road
London
w6 8jb

The Collins website address is:
www.collins.co.uk

Collins is a registered trademark of
HarperCollins Publishers Ltd.

First published in 2005

A catalogue record for this book is available from the British Library.
ISBN 0 00 720768 9

Commissioning Editor: Helen Brocklehurst
Art Director: Mark Thomson
Editor: Rosamund Kidman-Cox
Design and layout: Richard Marston
Proofreader: Kate Parker
Index: Hilary Bird
Editorial Assistant: Julia Koppitz

Colour reproduction by Dot Gradation, Essex
Printed and bound in Italy by LEGO, Vicenza

Contents

Introduction

Extreme Nature is about some of the most intriguing, supernatural, out of the ordinary and extreme plants and animals on the planet. A fish that can change sex, a frog that gives birth through its mouth and a flower that smells so bad it makes people faint are in the motley collection of weird and wonderful creatures included in the book.

If proof were ever needed that fact really is stranger than fiction, then look no further than the natural world. Did you know, for example, that a bombardier beetle can blast a chemical spray that's as hot as boiling water? Are you aware that a castor bean produces a toxin 6,000 times more deadly than cyanide? And have you ever wondered about the three-toed sloth, which has just two modes of being: asleep and not quite asleep?

It would have been hard for a science fiction writer to dream up some of the most bizarre creatures and wacky behaviour described in this book. Imagine an animal that squirts up to a quarter of its own blood at its predators – that's the Texas horned lizard. There is a frog that can withstand being frozen to −270°C (−454°F) and a moth with a 35cm (14in) tongue. A fish that can inflate itself to become a spine-covered sphere three times its original size may sound like a character from *The Hitchhiker's Guide to the Galaxy*, but it really does exist, in tropical seas around the world, in the form of the pufferfish.

One of the richest environments for such peculiar and eccentric wildlife is the sea. This is where scientists first discovered the coelacanth, for example – a strange-looking fish that was thought to have gone extinct 65 million years ago, but is now known to be alive and well and living in the western Indian Ocean. The sea is where we first set eyes on a remarkable octopus that lives a life of deception, by disguising itself as anything from a flounder or a jellyfish to a sea snake. And in the cold, dark ocean depths scientists have found shrimp-like creatures thriving 11 km (6.8 miles) below sea level. But the sea is also the most unexplored region of the world and studying its wildlife can be about as difficult and challenging as exploring outer space. Even now, there are probably huge animals lurking beneath the ocean waves as yet unseen by human eyes – and untold numbers of smaller ones. But with the help of space-age research techniques and equipment, such as deep-sea submersibles and remote-access vehicles, we are just beginning to understand the true extent of alien-like life on our own planet.

There are more outlandish creatures to discover on land, too, though many of them are likely to be the natural world's tiddlers and relatively hard to find. But the fact that we've already unearthed plants that eat animals, insects capable of walking on water and frogs with baggy skin just makes scientists determined to search for new species of plants and animals and ever-more extravagant forms of behaviour. It's hard not to wonder what secrets have yet to be unravelled in the treetops, deep underground, in hidden corners of remote tropical rainforests, or under the glare of a microscope.

Extreme Nature was written with the invaluable help of over 150 such scientists working in all corners of the globe. With their generous assistance, in just a few sentences it's been possible to summarise some of the highlights of many years, sometimes decades, of research. Thanks to them, if you've ever wondered which animal has the best colour vision, if a millipede really does have a thousand legs, how fast a falcon can swoop, or which is the world's most dangerous snake, this is the place to look.

Any study of extreme nature is inevitably full of surprises, and when it comes to superlatives, there is always another record-breaker just around the corner. But while there's little doubt that few of the records we've included are absolutes, in one way or another all animals and plants have something exceptional about them that deserves our attention. It's certainly been enormous fun corresponding with so many experts in so many different fields and, with their guidance, making the final selection.

Ultimately, the aim of the book is simply to revel in these other-worldly creatures and their outlandish behaviour. We hope you enjoy being wowed by some of their exploits.

Extreme

Abilities

Most devious plant · Strangest boxer · Most explosive defence
Most poisonous animal · Most ingenious tool-maker · Most gruesome
partnership · Best electro-detector · Stickiest skin · Deadliest plant
Biggest blood-sucker · Keenest sense of smell · Most enthusiastic singer
Most gruesome tongue · Most inquisitive bird · Biggest drug-user · Most painful
stinger · Slipperiest plant · Heaviest drinker · Best mimic · Most formidable
killer · Best architect · Most painful tree · Loudest bird call · Deadliest drooler
Most sensitive slasher · Smelliest plant · Most impressive comeback
Hottest animal · Most shocking animal · Coldest animal · Most talkative animal
Most bizarre defence · Smelliest animal · Slimiest animal · Keenest hearing
Stickiest spitter · Best colour vision · Most dangerous snake

Most devious plant

The natural world as we know it is built on partnerships. But in all societies there are cheats, and plants are no exception. Most green plants would be unable to exist without the help of fungi, which provide them with food-exchange partnerships. In fact, the invasion of the land by plants – algae – was probably only made possible by such partnerships. It has even been suggested that early land plants developed roots just so they could join forces with the fungal roots, or hyphae.

Most plants are proper partners, giving the carbohydrates they manufacture with their chlorophyll. Some, notably orchids, have such a close partnership that they don't even bother to produce proper food packages to accompany their embryos into the world, instead relying on fungi in the soil to provide the food needed for germination and early growth. This allows an orchid to produce lightweight, microscopic seeds – millions of them.

Some orchids, however, have become cheats: they use fungi that have partnerships with trees, and they never give anything in exchange. Via fungal hyphae, these orchid vampires tap into the trees, siphoning off nutrients. The give-away is often the fact that they have stopped producing chlorophyll and so aren't green but a rather sickly pinkish cream, like the ghost orchid, or brown, like the bird's-nest orchid. Some, such as western coralroot, are blood red or even purple. The drawback is that, without the fungus, the orchid will die. And one day a fungus might just evolve a way to get its own back.

NAME **ghost orchid** *Epipogium aphyllum*
LOCATION North and Central Europe east to Japan
ABILITY cheating a fungus

Mutual relationships in the sea are common. A famous one is between a hermit crab and an anemone, where the former gains protection from the anemone's stinging nematocysts, and the latter gets leftover food. Boxer crabs seem to have taken this a stage further. These tiny crabs – their carapace measures just 1.5cm (0.6in) – are prey to many animals. Their defence is to wield minute, stinging anemones on specialised claws. A jab with a 'glove' can cause pain (even to a human) or death and seems an effective defence – one boxer has even been observed seeing off a blue-ringed octopus. The anemones are also used in crab-to-crab boxing. But such fights are ritualistic, and boxing opponents hardly ever touch each other with their anemones, grappling instead with their walking legs.

When a growing boxer has to moult, it must put down its anemones and then grab them again when its new carapace (outer covering) has hardened. If it then finds itself with just one anemone, it merely breaks it in two, and the anemone obligingly duplicates itself. Surprisingly, the anemones don't seem to object to being picked up or to being brandished in the face of a predator – at least, one hasn't been seen trying to escape. And it's hard to tell what it gets in return other than free travel, but since the boxer uses the anemone to stun food animals, maybe the anemone gets enough leftovers to make life on the claw worth it.

Strangest boxer

NAME	**boxer crab**, or **pom pom crab**, *Lybia* species
LOCATION	Indian and Pacific Oceans
ABILITY	packing a punch with anemone gloves

In the world of insects, ants can overcome almost anything. But they don't always have it their own way. Bombardier beetles deliver an anti-ant surprise that is positively explosive. An ant, a spider or any other predator that, say, clamps on to a beetle's leg with hostile intent instantly finds itself blasted with a chemical spray that's as hot as boiling water.

So how does a small, cold-blooded creature manage to do this? Pure chemistry: in the rear of its abdomen are two identical glands lying side by side and opening at the abdominal tip. Each has an inner chamber containing hydrogen peroxide and hydroquinones and an outer one with catalase and peroxidase. When chemicals in the inner chamber are forced through the outer one, the chemicals react together, and the beetle has effectively created a bomb.

The resulting vapour, now containing the irritants known as p-benzoquinones, explodes from the end of the abdomen with a bang that's audible to a human and a temperature that's scalding to the would-be predator. What's more, the beetle can rotate its abdomen through 270 degrees in any direction, so that it can aim with absolute precision, and if 270 degrees isn't enough, it can shoot over its back, hitting a pair of reflectors that will ricochet the spray at the extra angle needed. Scientists find bombardiers fascinating because they're the only animals known to mix chemicals to create an explosion.

Most explosive defence

NAME **bombardier beetles** Carabidae family
LOCATION on every continent except Antarctica
ABILITY mixing chemicals to create an explosion

Most poisonous animal

NAME **golden poison-dart frog**
Phyllobates terribilis

LOCATION Pacific rainforests of Colombia, South America

ABILITY producing the most deadly poison of any animal

This tiny frog uses toxic chemicals as a defence in its body and is therefore technically poisonous (venomous animals inject toxins via a weapon – a tail, fang, spine, spur or tooth). The toxin is effective only when the frog is attacked, and since the frog doesn't want to be harmed, it sports a brilliant yellow or orange colour to warn predators of extreme danger.

In fact, this most poisonous of frogs is possibly the most poisonous animal in the world. The toxin is in its skin – you can die even by touching it – and there is enough in the skin of one animal to kill up to 100 people. Though the frog has been known to science only since 1978, inhabiting just one area in Colombia, the Chocó indians have known about it for generations, using its skin-gland secretions to poison their blowgun darts and kill animals in seconds.

The golden poison-dart frog gets most of its batrachotoxin (meaning frog poison) from other animals, probably small beetles, which in turn get it from plant sources. Captive-bred frogs, by comparison, never become toxic, presumably because they aren't fed toxic insects. The frog is active in the day, having few predators except a snake, that has become immune to the toxin. Surprisingly, birds have been discovered in New Guinea with the same batrachotoxin in their skin and feathers. The likely link has been tracked down to a small beetle, similar to the New World beetles, which also contains batrachotoxins.

Most ingenious tool-maker

NAME **New Caledonian crow** *Corvus moneduloides*

LOCATION Pacific island of New Caledonia

ABILITY thinking up ways to get at hard-to-reach food

Quite a few non-human animals, from sea otters to woodpecker finches, use tools and sometimes even craft them. It's usually assumed that the animal that is best at this is our nearest relative, the chimpanzee. Chimps use rocks to crack nuts and cut and fashion twigs or blades of grass to fish in mounds for termites. These are 'cultural' skills, practised only by certain groups of chimps and taught to youngsters. The skills are certainly sophisticated: an anthropologist once spent several months with a group of chimps trying to learn the art of termite fishing and finally achieved the proficiency, he reckoned, of a four-year-old chimp novice.

For pure innate, instant ingenuity, though, it would be hard to top the New Caledonian crow. In an experiment in a lab, meat was put in a little basket at the bottom of a perspex cylinder – and a female crow, Betty, was given a straight piece of wire. Holding the wire in her beak, she tried to pull the basket up, and failed. Then she took the wire to the side of the box holding the cylinder, poked it behind some tape and bent the end into a hook. She went back, hooked the basket, and got the meat. When the experiment was repeated, Betty did roughly the same thing, but with the addition of two different tool-making techniques. In the wild, New Caledonia crows make food-hooks out of twigs, by snipping off all but one protuberance. But bending a piece of wire . . . how would a crow know?

Most gruesome partnership

NAME	**luminescent bacteria** *Photorhabdus luminescens* meets **nematode** *Heterorhabditis bacteriophora*
LOCATION	inside a caterpillar or maggot
ABILITY	combining forces to eat larvae alive

This is a slow and horrible way to die. A worm-like creature, a nematode, goes on the hunt by squirming through the soil in search of an unsuspecting insect grub, or larva. It's not particularly fussy and likes anything from a weevil to a fly maggot, but it may take months to find a suitable victim. When it does, it penetrates the cuticle of the larva, either through an opening such as a breathing pore or by hacking a hole with its special 'tooth'. Once inside, it sets free more than a hundred bacteria from inside its gut, which start producing deadly toxins, digestive enzymes and antibiotics.

The bacteria are luminescent, and as they multiply, the grub takes on a deathly glow. The nematode then starts feeding on the bacteria and the remains of the grub corpse, which is kept free from other competing microorganisms by the antibiotics. Finally, it changes into a hermaphrodite female, laying eggs in the cadaver that hatch into both male and female nematodes.

Yet more of her eggs develop inside her, and when they hatch, the juvenile nematodes eat their mother. They then mate and produce their own eggs. It's at this point, two weeks later, that the grub finally breaks up and thousands of young nematodes (each carrying the bacteria in their guts) exit into the soil. The bacteria and the nematode can't exist without each other – a gruesome partnership but one that humans have joined, helping the little nematodes spread by deliberately releasing them to hunt down garden pests.

All sharks can, to some extent, detect other creatures by sensing the minuscule amount of electricity they create simply by virtue of being alive. In most sharks, this sense is principally an adjunct to more dominant senses (usually hearing, smell and vision) and is particularly important in the final split-second of an attack. But for hammerheads, it's the main thing, and it could be one reason why their heads are shaped in the curious way they are.

Sharks have special electrical receptors – hundreds of tiny, dark pores called 'ampullae of Lorenzini' – which are filled with a conductive gel that transfers electrical impulses to a nerve end in each pore. Ordinary sharks have these all over the snout and lower jaw, forming a curious pattern of dark holes resembling a sparse five-o'clock shadow.

But hammerheads also have a mass of them across the underside of their oblong heads, which scan across the sandy sea-bottom like metal detectors, searching for prey animals that can't be found in any other way – creatures such as stingrays and flatfish that bury themselves, lie still and usually have no appreciable scent.

The hammerheads are able to detect the slight direct currents caused by interaction between the bodies of their prey and the seawater and the even slighter alternating currents caused by muscle contractions around an animal's heart. The eight species of hammerhead can sense it better than most other sharks, and the biggest of these, the great hammerhead, which measures up to 6m (20ft) long, may be able to sense it best of all.

Best electro-detector

NAME	**great hammerhead** *Sphyrna mokarran*
LOCATION	tropical and warm temperate seas
SKILL	hunting with electricity

Stickiest skin

Some of the world's strangest creatures are found in Australia – a continent of extremes giving rise to extreme adaptations. The holy-cross toad lives where many other amphibians can't: in hot, harsh areas inland, where droughts may last for several years. It uses its strong back legs to burrow down in the soil, where it sits out the heat of the day, and when drought sets in, it survives by digging a chamber a metre or so underground in which it aestivates (becomes dormant), emerging only when the rains return.

Like its close toad relatives, the holy-cross also has unique glands in its skin. If it is disturbed or distressed, these release a special secretion that turns into glue. The glue hardens in seconds and has a tensile strength five times that of other natural glues. This is particularly useful should ants attack, as even the biggest immediately get stuck to the toad's skin. And since, like all frogs and toads, it sheds its skin and eats it about once a week, the holy-cross toad has the pleasure of swallowing the ants that attack it.

Scientists in Australia are now trying to produce an artificial glue as good as the toad's. Holy-cross toad glue will stick plastic, glass, cardboard and even metal together. More importantly, it can repair splits in cartilage and other body tissues and therefore might prove to be a miracle adhesive that will help surgeons repair the most difficult of injuries.

NAME **holy-cross**, **crucifix** or **Catholic toad**
Notaden bennetti
LOCATION Australia
ABILITY producing a super 'superglue'

Deadliest plant

The castor bean plant produces possibly the most deadly plant toxin, 6,000 times more deadly than cyanide, but it has also been known for thousands of years as a wonder plant. The secret and the poison both lie in the seed. More than 50 per cent of it comprises a rich oil, but to protect it from being eaten is ricin, a protein toxic to almost all animals (lesser quantities of ricin occur in the leaves). The poison, once ingested, inactivates the key protein-making elements of a cell without which it can't maintain itself and dies.

For humans, death is prolonged, ending in convulsions and failure of the liver and other organs. There is no known antidote. The most usual cause of poisoning comes from accidentally eating seeds, but ricin can be administered in aerosol form, in food or water, or injected, as in the famous case of a dissident Bulgarian journalist. While waiting at a bus stop at Waterloo station in London, in 1978, Georgi Markov was murdered by being stabbed with an umbrella that injected a pellet containing ricin. Widely available and easily produced, ricin could be used for biological warfare.

It is equally easy to extract the seed's valuable oil, however, which has been used for at least 4,000 years as a lamp oil and soap and also as medicine for a huge array of ailments. Today its uses include high-grade lubricants, textile dyes, printing ink, waxes, polishes, candles and crayons. In the future, its array of protective chemicals may even provide a cure for tumours.

NAME	**castor bean** *Ricinus communis*
LOCATION	worldwide; origin unknown, but probably Ethiopia
ABILITY	producing the deadly poison ricin

No, the biggest blood-sucker isn't a vampire bat. Vampires, which are native to the tropical Americas, don't actually suck blood – they lap it up. They find large mammals – most noticeably cows, pigs or horses – make a cut in their skin and then drink the blood. Not being very big (average body length is 6.5–9cm/2.5–3.5in), a single bat only actually consumes a few tablespoons of blood a night, though because of the anticoagulant in its saliva, the prey keeps bleeding for some time after the bat has flown away.

The world's largest leech, measuring up to 46cm (18ins) does suck blood, however, and a very hungry one can take in four times its body weight before it becomes satiated. Since a large Amazon leech weighs about 50g (1.8oz) – the record is 80g (2.8oz) – that's a lot more than a few teaspoons of blood. Like the vampire, the Amazon leech feeds on large mammals, which it attacks when they enter water, and it also uses an anticoagulant to keep the animal's blood flowing. But the leech injects an anaesthetic, too, so that the temporary host is unaware of what's happening to it.

All leeches are segmented worms – their nearest relatives are earthworms – and all, regardless of size, have precisely 32 segments. A few segments at each end of the Amazon leech are modified into suckers for attaching to prey, and every segment has its own independent nerve centre – hence a leech has 32 brains.

Biggest blood-sucker

NAME **Amazon leech** *Haementeria ghilianii*

LOCATION Amazon basin

ABILITY drinking up to four times its weight in blood

Keenest sense of smell

Many animals rely on their sense of smell to find food or a mate and even to find their way around. Some live in places where other senses are of little use – eyes don't help much if you spend most of your life in the dark, and ears would be hopeless in a particularly noisy environment – so they rely on smell more than most.

Some animals, such as sharks, are selective in their smelling abilities and are super-sensitive to significant smells that are relevant to activities such as feeding or breeding. In fact, smell is so important to sharks that they have been dubbed 'swimming noses'. Their smell receptors are fine-tuned to picking up small concentrations of fish extract, blood and other chemicals – but so are the receptors of many other animals. Some catfish have such super-receptors that they can smell compounds at 1 part to 10 billion parts of water.

The likelihood is, though, that moths are the record-holders, especially the males. They use their antennae to home in on the sex pheromones, or chemical allures, released by females and can even detect if these females are on plants suitable for egg-laying. Some females release deviously small amounts of pheromone, to make sure that only those males with the most highly tuned antennae can follow the trails. The likely record-holder for the best *known* sense of smell is the polyphemus moth: just one pheromone molecule landing on a male's antennae will trigger a response in his brain.

NAME	**polyphemus moth** *Antheraea polyphemus*
LOCATION	North America
ABILITY	a male can detect a female on the evidence of just one molecule

Drop a hydrophone into the water in an area where humpback whales are breeding and you may hear a baffling medley of moans, groans, roars, snores, squeaks and whistles. These are the hauntingly beautiful sounds made by male humpbacks, which are famous for singing the longest and most complex of animal songs. Since most singing takes place at the breeding grounds, it is probably used to woo females and to warn away rival males – but the songs may also have more subtle meanings and nuances that we do not yet understand.

A song can last for as long as half an hour, and as soon as the whale has finished, it often goes back to the beginning and sings it all over again. Each song consists of several main components, or phrases, which are always sung in the same order and repeated a number of times, but are forever being refined and improved. All the humpbacks in one area sing broadly the same song, incorporating each other's improvisations as they go along. This means that the song heard one day is different from the one being heard several months later and, in this way, the entire composition changes over a period of several years.

Meanwhile, humpback whales in other oceans sing very different compositions. They probably all croon about the same trials and tribulations in life, but the differences are so distinctive that experts can tell where a whale was recorded simply by listening to the intricacies of its own special song.

Most enthusiastic singer

NAME	**humpback whale** *Megaptera novaeangliae*
LOCATION	oceans worldwide
ABILITY	singing the longest and most complex songs in the animal kingdom

Most gruesome tongue

This is probably the world's most specialised and gruesome isopod – one of a group of crustaceans including woodlice, marine gribbles and slaters. Most isopods lead perfectly normal lives as herbivores, scavengers or carnivores, but some are parasites. *Cymothoa exigua* has a tendancy to select the mouth of the spotted rose snapper fish for its hangout.

Latching on to the fish's tongue with its hooked legs (pereopods), it feeds on mucus, blood and tissue, gradually eating away the tongue. Gripping onto the tongue stub, the isopod then effectively becomes the fish's tongue, growing as its host grows and feeding on particles of meat that float free as the fish eats. The biggest individual isopod recorded was 39mm (1.5in), but presumably it can grow to be as big as the fish needs its tongue to be.

Perhaps the practice is not as gruesome as it looks, as the rose snapper can continue to feed, but no one knows whether a time comes when *Cymothoa* decides to let go and get a taste of blood in someone else's mouth. Strangely, the relationship between the fish and its parasite has been observed only in the Gulf of California, or Sea of Cortez, though the fish is found in the eastern Pacific, from Mexico to Peru. It is the only known example of a parasite replacing not just a host's organ but also its function (to hold prey) – a hard act to swallow.

NAME   **isopod** *Cymothoa exigua*
SIZE   up to 4 cm long
ABILITY   eating and then mimicking the tongue of the spotted rose snapper fish

Most inquisitive bird

NAME **kea** *Nestor notabilis*

LOCATION New Zealand

ABILITY curiosity

Parrots are highly inquisitive, but even among parrots, keas are exceptional. They're native to New Zealand's South Island, a cold, snowy, unparrotlike place where keas have to use all their wits to find a meal. While parrots elsewhere are flying from one conspicuous fruit to another, keas are searching under rocks and bark and in bushes, cones and shells for food such as roots, shoots, berries or insect larvae. This and a mountainous habitat virtually free of predators has, over 2.5 million years of evolution, made them insatiably curious. And they're especially drawn to things they've never seen before. So when humans arrived in New Zealand, the keas were delivered a bonanza of new objects to investigate for food.

Nowadays great sources of fascination are camping grounds and ski-resorts. These parrots are large and have powerful beaks, and they can rip right through a canvas tent for the sheer joy of investigation. A particular favourite is the rubber on cars – windscreen wipers mainly. One gang of keas is said to have ripped out the rubber lining around the windscreen of a tourists' hire car, causing the glass to fall inwards and opening up the interior. When the tourists returned, they found clothes, food and car parts scattered in the snow, while the keas appeared to be playing a game of football with an empty Coke can. The birds then retreated and watched – with great curiosity, it seemed – to see what the tourists would do about it.

Biggest drug-user

NAME **chimpanzee** *Pan troglodytes*

LOCATION forests in East, West and Central Africa

ABILITY self-medication

Yes, humans are the biggest drug-users. But we are not the only ones who use drugs, and we are only just beginning to discover the pharmaceutical knowledge of other animals. The current top-of-the-list user is the chimpanzee. Like us, chimps get stomach ache from time to time after overeating or consuming toxins. They also get parasites and diseases, and stressed animals usually end up feeling pretty ill.

It's not surprising that an intelligent primate such as a chimp, which learns by trial and error and example, should have started to use medicinal products, since their forest habitat is full of them. In Tanzania, chimps suffering from diarrhoea have been seen using the leaves of the 'bitter leaf' tree that local people know as a medicine for malaria, amoebic dysentery and intestinal worms. Across Africa, chimps have been seen seeking out rough-leafed plants, plucking whole leaves from them, carefully folding the leaves, rolling them around in their mouths and then swallowing them. Excreted whole, the leaves push out parasites such as intestinal worms.

Many other animals also appear to self-medicate. Capuchin monkeys have been seen rubbing their fur with pungent plants that contain healing and insect-repellant properties. Black lemurs rub insect-killing chemicals from millipedes onto their fur. An elephant has been observed seeking out labour-inducing leaves of a tree just before giving birth. Given our increasing need for new antibiotics and remedies, such examples provide a good reason to keep nature's pharmacy intact by respecting the environment.

Some say this is the world's most venomous animal, but this depends what you mean. Is it the venomous creature you are most likely to encounter, does it kill more people than any other, or are the chemicals most toxic? Certainly, a single box jellyfish contains enough venom to kill at least 60 people, and many do die after being stung.

Though the jellyfish has no desire to kill humans, it is a hunter. An adult box jellyfish – as large as a human head, with tentacles up to 4.6m (15ft) long – has a full array of powerful stinging cells, called nematocysts, and hunts mainly fish. It is very active (unlike many other jellyfish) and jet-propels itself through the sea in search of prey. It's also transparent, ensuring that fish (and humans) don't spot its deadly tentacles.

There are four bundles of about ten tentacles, most over 2m (6ft 6in) long and each carrying around 3 million nematocysts. The toxin contains chemicals that affect heart muscle and nerves and destroy tissue, the purpose being to kill a fish quickly so it doesn't get away. But if a box jellyfish encounters a human, it may also sting in self-defence. The pain is excruciating, and without anti-venom, a victim can die from heart failure in just a few minutes. In addition, nematocysts fire not just on command but when stimulated physically or chemically. Strangely, they can't penetrate women's tights, and until 'stinger suits' became available, lifesavers patrolling beaches would wear tights unashamedly.

Most painful stinger

NAME **box jellyfish** *Chironex fleckeri*
LOCATION near-shore waters of parts of Australia and South-east Asia
ABILITY causing excruciating pain and possible death

Slipperiest plant

NAME **pitcher plants** *Nepenthes* species
LOCATION South-east Asia
ABILITY catching prey in slippery, deadly pitchers

There are many different species of pitcher plant, but all are insect-traps with the slipperiest of sides, providing extra nitrogen (from insect corpses) to help the plants flower and set seed. Among the most sophisticated are the leaves of vine-like *Nepenthes*. Each of these pitfall traps has an 'umbrella' lid and a base partly filled with a soup of digestive enzymes. The lure may be colour (usually red), smell (nectar or, later, rotting corpses) or tasty hairs. When an insect lands on the rim, it slips into the deadly broth, possibly intoxicated by narcotic nectar.

Slipperiness is achieved in two ways, perhaps depending on what insects are likely to be attracted (walking insects if the *Nepenthes* is on the ground or flying insects if it is up in the tree canopy). The inner walls are usually impossible to climb, being covered with slippery waxy platelets. Others go a stage further and have a surface that attracts a film of water which aquaplanes the insects to their death. Some also use trickery. When their pitchers are dry, ants are lured by the nectar, and don't slip, and so go and tell more ants about the find. If the surface is wet when they return, they all fall in.

Another of the *Nepenthes* species is in partnership with an ant that has specialised feet, allowing it to get in and out of the pitcher to retrieve corpses. It eats these and drops the remains and its faeces into the pitcher, so speeding up the release of nitrogen for its predatory host to ingest.

To say this or any other hummingbird drinks like a fish is to understate how much it drinks. In proportion to its body weight, it drinks a lot more than a fish. (Just to get that cliché straight: freshwater fish don't drink – they absorb water through their skin. Saltwater fish that drink don't do so to excess.) In the case of the hummingbird, it's the fault of the flowers. Hummingbirds have evolved to drink nectar. The flowers they visit have evolved to provide that nectar, and the nectar they provide is typically about 30 per cent sugar and the rest water. To keep their wings going at a rate quicker than the human eye can see – to hover – hummingbirds need a huge amount of sugar, which means that by drinking nectar they take in up to five times their body weight in water every day.

If any other animal, including a human, tried to drink even one times its body weight, it would be dead long before it could do it. So while hummingbirds were evolving beaks to fit into the flowers with their watered-down nectar, they were also having to evolve nature's heaviest-duty kidneys. Some water just passes through the bird unprocessed, but 80 per cent goes to the kidneys to be expelled as very dilute urine. And why the broad-tailed in particular? It's simply the most energetic hummingbird, and thus the most supersaturated.

Heaviest drinker

NAME	**broad-tailed hummingbird** *Selasphorus platycercus*
LOCATION	North America
ABILITY	can drink up to five times its body weight in a day

Best mimic

NAME   **Indo-Malayan mimic octopus**

LOCATION   Indonesian-Malaysian archipelago

ABILITY   pretending to be anything but an octopus

If you are a medium-sized predator, the average octopus is one of the most edible animals in the sea. It's substantial and meaty, and without a shell, bones, spines, poisons or any other unpleasant defence mechanisms. In fact, the best defence most species of octopus have is to stay hidden as much as possible and do their own hunting at night.

So to find one in full view in the shallows in daylight was a surprise for two Australian underwater photographers, swimming off the Indonesian island of Flores in the early 1990s. Actually, what they saw at first was a flounder. It was only when they looked again that they saw a medium-sized octopus, with all eight of its arms folded and its two eyes staring upwards to create the illusion of a fishy body. An octopus has a big brain, excellent eyesight and the ability to change colour and pattern, and this one was using these assets to turn itself into a completely different creature.

Many more of this species have been found since then, and there are now photographs of octopuses that could be said to be morphing into sea snakes (six arms down a hole, and two undulating menacingly), hermit crabs, stingrays, crinoids, holothurians, snake eels, brittlestars, ghost crabs, mantis shrimp, blennies, jawfish, jellyfish, lionfish and sand anemones. And while they mimic, they hunt – producing the spectacle of, say, a flounder suddenly developing an octopodian arm, sticking it down a hole and grabbing whatever's hiding there.

Anything that can attack and kill the largest animal that ever lived, the blue whale (see p.198), has to be the greatest predator ever (apart, of course, from *Homo sapiens*). But blue whales are peaceable creatures with few defences apart from size, and so maybe the killer whale qualifies better on the grounds that it can kill the great white shark. At a maximum length of 9m (29ft 6in), killer whales are the largest members of the dolphin family and among the largest of all predators, but their real edge is that they're pack hunters and work together to subdue large prey.

Several distinct forms are known – residents, transients and offshores – each of which differ significantly in appearance, behaviour, group size and diet. The transients are the ones that tend to specialise in larger prey but, perhaps surprisingly, they travel in smaller groups than their fish-eating relatives: fewer than six or seven is fairly typical (fish-eating groups often comprise 15–30 whales). The transients devise different, often ingenious, hunting techniques for different prey. In the Antarctic, for example, they will tip seals and penguins off ice floes and into the mouths of their group-mates; and in Patagonia, they beach themselves to grab sealion pups.

When Basque whalers saw killer whales feeding on the carcasses of dead whales, they called them 'whale killers', and the name stuck. Many people prefer to use the more politically correct name, orca, but in Latin, *orcus* means 'belonging to the kingdom of the dead', and so it's not much better.

Most formidable killer

NAME	**killer whale**, or **orca**, *Orcinus orca*
LOCATION	oceans worldwide
ABILITY	preying on the world's largest animals

Best architect

NAME   **African termite** *Macrotermes bellicosus*

LOCATION   sub-Saharan Africa

ABILITY   creating an air-conditioned, multi-storey communal residence

Some 200 species of ant – most famously leafcutter ants – farm fungus inside their nests as a source of fast food. So do about 3,500 beetles and 330 species of termite. But of all these insects, none seems to cultivate a more difficult crop than the African termite, and no crop requires more elaborate technology to maintain it. The staple fungus of African termites grows only on their faeces and needs a very particular temperature. Anything above or below 30.1°C (86°F) is too hot or too cold, and every aspect of the construction of the termite mound is part of an effort to keep the temperature exactly that.

The termites always build with mud, above a damp pit. They dig at least two long boreholes down to the water table. They also construct a 3m (10ft) diameter cellar, about 1m (3.3ft) deep, with a thick central pillar that supports the main part of the mound. This houses the queen, the nursery and the fungus farms. On the ceiling of the cellar are thin, circular condensation veins, and around the sides of the mound are ventilation ducts. On top are hollow towers – chimneys – that rise 6m (20ft) above ground level. Every dimension is just right for the precise circulation of air and moisture that will keep the fungus at 30.1°C no matter what it's like outside. What's more, workers are only a maximum of 2cm (0.8in) in size, and so in relative terms, the mound is taller than any human building – the equivalent of 180 storeys.

Of course, any tree could fall on you, and plenty of trees are poisonous to eat, but this aside, the trees that cause the most excruciating pain are ones that you just brush against. These are the stinging trees that are found in several parts of the world but are most persistently painful in that land of advanced toxins, Australia. Here are six *Dendrocnide* species, two of which – the northern shiny-leaf stinging tree and the southern giant stinging tree – are large, tree-like trees, and four of which are more like shrubs. Of the six, the worst agony is said to be inflicted by a shrub, the gympie-gympie, but they all hurt a lot.

What looks at first like a layer of fur on all parts except the roots is really a mass of tiny glass (silicon) fibres containing toxic chemicals. Just a brush against a tree results in the skin being impaled with a scattering of fibres, which act like hypodermic needles and are all but impossible to extract (Australian first-aid kits sometimes include wax hair-removal strips). The poison causes burning, itching, swelling and sometimes blistering that is said to be at its most unbearable soon after contact but can keep causing pain for years. The fibres can penetrate most clothing, and sometimes air-borne ones can be inhaled. Oddly, the stings don't affect all animals. Insects and even some native mammals actually eat the leaves. The ones that suffer tend to be introductions to Australia, such as dogs, horses and humans.

Most painful tree

NAME	**gympie-gympie stinging tree** *Dendrocnide moroides*
LOCATION	Australia
ABILITY	defending itself with toxic chemicals

Loudest bird call

NAME   **kakapo** *Strigops habroptilus*
LOCATION   New Zealand
ABILITY   producing a boom that can be heard up to 5km (3 miles) away

Which bird is loudest depends on who is listening and where. The song of a nightingale overcoming traffic noise is so loud (90 decibels) that prolonged exposure to it could, theoretically, damage your ears. So could the even louder, shrill, 115-decibel cry of a male kiwi or the metallic 'bonks' of the Central American bellbird, designed to carry in thick rainforest. But possibly the best long-distance sound to make is a boom.

In Europe, the booming record-holder is the bittern. But the world record-holder is probably the New Zealand kakapo, which is now extinct on the two main islands and, despite great conservation efforts, numbers fewer than 90 individuals. Every three or four years, the normally solitary males gather at traditional kakapo amphitheatres – display grounds with excavated bowls. Here they puff up air sacs in their chest and belly and start booming, an average of 1,000 times an hour for 6–7 hours a night (kakapos are nocturnal, and sound carries best in the colder night air). They do this for 3–4 months to call in likely mates to witness their dance displays and for mating. But since this giant, flightless parrot is now confined to a handful of offshore islands, few people will ever hear its eerie, 'fog-horn' boom.

Intriguingly, the booms of Australasian cassowaries are nearly as loud but have an added long-distance element: a low-frequency component below the range of our hearing (though it can be felt). It's likely that a kakapo boom also contains ultra-low-frequency sound, but its booming is now so rare that it has yet to be completely analysed.

Deadliest drooler

The Komodo dragon is a renowned giant: the average male is more than 2.2m (7ft 5in) long, and some measure up to 3.1m (10ft 2in). The longest lizard of all, however, is its much slimmer relative, the Salvadori monitor from New Guinea, though two thirds of its 2.7m (8ft 8in) maximum length is made up by its tail.

But the Komodo dragon is the heaviest lizard of all, with an average weight of 60kg (130lb) and a maximum of 80kg (176lb), and it is a fearsome predator. It has large, sharp, serrated teeth for cutting and tearing prey, but its hidden weapon is its bacteria-laden saliva. Once bitten, a victim may escape, but within a few days it will succumb to infection. The dragon then tracks it down with its acute sense of smell – a sense that also makes it a super-efficient scavenger.

Though it is a giant by today's standards, the Komodo dragon may be a pygmy compared to one of its mainland ancestors (Flores Island supported other 'pygmies', including a now-extinct elephant, on which the dragon is believed to have preyed). In Australia there once existed a true giant, the 6.9m (23ft), 617kg (1,370lb) monster monitor *Megalania prisca*, which became extinct about 40,000 years ago. The Komodo dragon poses relatively little threat to humans and usually only bites when cornered. But *Megalania*, whether or not it was a deadly drooler, would have been a lizard to be very, very afraid of.

NAME	**Komodo dragon** *Varanus komodoensis*
LOCATION	islands of Komodo, Rinca, Gili Motang, Gili Dasami and Flores, Indonesia
ABILITY	producing dangerous bacteria-laden saliva

A sawfish has external teeth, set around a sensitive, flat snout – the saw, or rostrum (here shown from the underside). Swung from side to side, the saw can be used as a powerful weapon to slash shoaling fish such as mullet and herring, which it then eats off the sea-bottom. Generally speaking, though, the sawfish is a slow and peaceable animal, spending its time in shallow, muddy water, raking the mud with its saw for crustaceans and other prey. The saw-teeth get worn by all this grubbing, but they grow continuously from their bases and so don't wear out.

Like its close relatives, the rays, it's perfectly camouflaged against the bottom of the sea, and like its more distant relatives, the sharks, it swims in an undulating way. And like both groups, its hard bits are cartilage, not bone, and its teeth are adapted scales. It has another similarity. Using special cells, the 'ampullae of Lorenzini', on its saw and head, it can detect electrical fields generated by prey.

One problem for females is that they give birth to live saw-babies. But a youngster's saw is covered with a sheath to make birth relatively painless. A much greater problem for all sawfish (possibly seven species) is the fact that their coastal waters are being polluted and developed and that they have been overfished to the point where all are endangered, some critically. A sawfish's saw is also its downfall. Not only has it been sought after as a trophy, but it also fatally entangles the fish in nets.

Most sensitive slasher

NAME **sawfish** *Pristis* species

LOCATION shallow, warm coastal waters

ABILITY using its saw for slashing and sifting

What smells bad to us often doesn't bother other animals. In fact, the scent of the foul-smelling titan arum – the tallest and probably heaviest of flowering structures – is positively attractive to carrion beetles and bees. Whether its smell is the worst, to us, has still to be tested (there are other contenders for this, including the even bigger giant titan, *A. gigas*). But the titan arum produces a sufficiently awful smell to make people faint.

The 'flower', or inflorescence, comprises a vase-shaped spathe (petal-like leaf) at least 1.2m (4ft) tall, which grows rapidly from a gigantic tuber weighing up to 80kg (177lb). Out of this rises a spadix, a spike with thousands of tiny flowers more than 2.4m (8ft) tall, so strange it gives the arum its scientific name: 'huge deformed penis'. The upper part of the spike produces the smell, and to make it travel further, the spadix generates heat and may steam at night as it pulses its fragrance of ammonia, rotting flesh and bad eggs for up to eight hours at a time.

This attracts pollinating, carrion-loving insects, but few people have observed the pollination, probably because the plant flowers only every 3–10 years and then for just two days. Once the flower dies and hornbills have dispersed its seeds, it's replaced by a titanic leaf up to 6m (20ft) tall, which makes the food so that, one day, the tuber can grow another stinking flower.

Smelliest plant

NAME	**titan arum**, **corpse flower**, or **devil's tongue**, *Amorphophallus titanum*
LOCATION	western Sumatra, Indonesia
ABILITY	pumping out the smell of decomposing flesh

Most impressive comeback

New Zealand's Chatham Islands are believed to have been the last Pacific archipelago to be visited by humans. Yet when people finally did visit, they stayed, and they did a pretty thorough job of doing what humans have always done to islands: stripped them of a lot of their native plants and animals. The Polynesians arrived around 700 years ago, the Europeans came along in the 1790s, and between them they caused the extinction of 26 of the islands' 68 species and subspecies of birds. The main cause was introduced land mammals, and among the sufferers from cats and rats in particular was the 15cm (6in) endemic black robin.

By 1900 it had disappeared from the two main islands and survived only on Little Mangere, a tiny, windswept stack with sheer cliffs that helped keep predators away but didn't offer the birds much protection from the elements. By 1972 only 18 were left. By 1976, seven.

In the meantime, though, the government had bought nearby Mangere Island and begun to reforest it, and all the birds were moved there. Nevertheless, by 1980, there were just five, with only one breeding pair. But by fostering eggs to other bird species on other islands – which improved the survival chances of the chicks and spurred the breeding female to nest again – conservationists painstakingly cranked the species back to life. Now there are about 250 black robins on Mangere and South East islands, and there are plans to repopulate other islands in the Chathams.

NAME **Chatham Island black robin** *Petroica traversi*
LOCATION Chatham Islands, east of South Island, New Zealand
ACHIEVEMENT increasing in numbers from just five to 250 in 18 years

Hottest animal

NAME **Pompeii worm** *Alvinella pompejana*
LOCATION deep-sea hydrothermal vents
ABILITY withstanding scalding water

The Pompeii worm thrives in large colonies in one of the darkest, deepest, most hellish places on Earth – close to a geyser of water so hot it could melt the worm in a second. It is also subject to a pressure great enough to crush a person and doused in a soup of toxic sulphur and heavy metals. Communities of Pompeii worms cling to the sides of 'smokers' 2–3 km (1.2–1.9 miles) under the sea. These belching chimneys grow over hydrothermal vents on volcanic mountain ranges, created from the chemicals that precipitate out as 300°C (572°F) vent water meets cold seawater.

To survive on a smoker requires super-worm strategies. For its home, the worm makes a paper-like chemical-and-heat-resistant tube. For a thermal blanket, it 'grows' a fleece of filamentous bacteria, feeding it with sugar-rich mucus secreted from its back. This blanket may also detoxify the vent fluid in its tube.

Unlike the vent tubeworm *Riftia pachyptila*, the Pompeii worm has a gut and 'lips' which it extends to 'graze' on bacteria that grow on the surface of the colony. But no one knows quite how it copes with what are the highest temperatures and temperature gradients experienced by any organism apart from bacteria, for though it angles its head (gills, mainly) away from the hottest water, its tail experiences flushes hotter than 80°C (176°F). Keen to make use of the Pompeii worm's technology for human endeavours, scientists are now racing against each other to unravel its survival secrets.

Most shocking animal

NAME	**electric eel** *Electrophorus electricus*
LOCATION	South American rivers
ABILITY	stunning prey with electrical discharges

Think of it as a living battery. The electric eel can grow to be more than 2m (6ft 5in) long, but its organs are packed just behind its head, leaving 80 per cent of its body to electricity generation. It's stacked with up to 6,000 specially adapted muscle cells, or electrocytes, aligned like cells in a battery. Each electrocyte emits low-voltage impulses that together can add up to 600 volts – enough to render a human unconscious. The positive pole is behind the eel's head, and the negative pole is at the tip of its tail. It tends to remain straight when swimming, using its long ventral fin for propulsion, and so keeps a uniform electric field around itself.

Electricity affects almost every bit of the eel's behaviour. As well as stunning or killing with high-voltage pulses, it communicates with other eels electrically and uses electrolocation (a sort of electrical bounce-back system) to detect objects and other creatures in the water. Fish and frogs are its staple prey, and it can detect the minute electric currents these and other living things produce. The eel can't see well, but this doesn't matter much, since it is mainly nocturnal and tends to live in murky water.

There are other electrified fish, including the related knifefishes, which generate a weak electric field around themselves that they use to sense objects and fish prey and to communicate. The only other shockers are the torpedo ray and the electric catfish, but neither is as shocking as the electric eel.

Coldest animal

There's an African midge so well adapted to drought conditions that, as a sideline, it can withstand being artificially frozen to −270°C (−454°F). Lots of other insects can survive freezing, too, but the creatures that can withstand cold for the longest period are probably bacteria in Antarctica.

The most freeze-tolerant higher animal is the wood frog, which can literally become a 'frog-sicle', enabling it to live further north than any other amphibian and to hibernate close to snowmelt ponds, presumably to give it a head start and enable it to reproduce quickly before the ponds dry.

When the temperature drops below freezing, the frog's liver starts converting glycogen to glucose, which acts as an antifreeze. The blood passes the glucose to the vital cells, which are then protected from freezing on the inside, all the way down to −8°C (18°F). But the rest of the frog's body fluids, up to 65 per cent of them, turn to ice and the organs, deprived of blood, actually stop working. Even the eyeballs and the brain freeze. It is effectively the living dead. (The painted turtle *Chrysemys picta* can do this, too, but only briefly.) When a thaw comes, the frog's heart starts beating and pumps blood containing clotting proteins around the body, which stops bleeding from wounds caused by the jagged ice crystals. The frogsicle quickly comes back to life and, just as miraculously, so do the frozen parasitic worms in its body.

NAME	**wood frog** *Rana sylvatica*
LOCATION	Canada and Alaska
ABILITY	withstanding being frozen for weeks

Most talkative animal

NAME **African grey parrot** *Psittacus erithacus*
LOCATION Central and West Africa
ABILITY communicating with humans

African greys live in huge flocks that sweep through the rainforests foraging for fruit, nuts, seeds and herbs and constantly communicating with each other. In the wild, no one has been able to do more than categorise their calls as, for example, threat or making contact. These calls could, though, be far more meaningful and complex if the language skills of pet grey parrots are anything to go by – for African greys can be taught to understand and speak human language and may some day even be able to read words.

The most famous of these parrots (though several others have been making the news recently) is Alex, protégé of Dr Irene Pepperberg of Brandeis University in Massachusetts. Alex can identify the colours and shapes of objects and what they're made of. He can, for instance, say, 'four-corner wood square' if that's what he's been shown. If he wants to be given something or to go somewhere, he only needs to ask. And he can actually make wisecracks and some rudimentary conversation.

One story Dr Pepperberg tells about him is how during a demonstration of his ability to identify alphabetic letters on cards, Alex would say 'sssss' for S, 'shhh' for SH, 'tuh' for T and so on and after each correct answer would ask for a nut. Since that would have slowed things down too much, Dr Pepperberg would say each time, 'Good birdie, but later.' Finally Alex looked at her, narrowed his eyes and said, 'Want a nut. Nnn, uh, tuh.'

Revered by native peoples for thousands of years, the Texas horned lizard has an array of abilities. It eats mainly ants – and lots of them, since much of an ant is indigestible. This necessitates a huge stomach. Eating more than 200 ants a day means exposure in the open for long periods, and being stomach-heavy means a horned lizard finds it difficult to scamper away from predators.

Instead, it relies on an armoury of defences. It has camouflage colouring, with an outline broken by spines and outgrowths, and it will freeze if a predator approaches. Its horns and spines can pierce the throat of a snake or bird, and it can hiss and blow itself up to look even more fearsome. When it comes to coyotes, foxes and dogs, a horned lizard's most spectacular defence is to squirt foul-tasting blood from sinuses behind its eyes. That usually has the desired effect. But it squirts only when it's provoked, since it risks losing up to a quarter of its blood.

Such abilities are, however, no defence against human invasion of its land. Its strange shape and colouring has made it attractive to reptile collectors, and its habit of freezing means it is prone to being run over. And with humans have come exotic fire ants, which it can't eat and which are replacing the native ants on which the lizard depends – a sorry way for such a determined survivor to go.

Most bizarre defence

NAME **Texas horned lizard** *Phrynosoma cornutum*
LOCATION southern USA and Mexico
ABILITY blood squirting

Bad smell is all in the nose of the receiver, and we humans have far fewer sensors than most animals. Nonetheless, we can smell a striped skunk up to 3.2km (2 miles) away, if the wind is in the right direction. It's possible to train our brains to ignore the most disgusting of smells, from vomit and faeces to rotting flesh – but never skunk. Other animals, including African zorillos, Tasmanian devils, wolverines and different species of skunk, produce revolting musk when threatened or attacked, but not of the strength or permanence of striped skunk spray.

The amber oil is made in two muscular glands under the skunk's tail and can be delivered as a spray or precision jet up to a distance of 3.6m (12ft). The spray contains compounds which are the cause of the vomit-producing smell, like very, very rotten eggs. It can also cause temporary blindness and, if swallowed, unconsciousness. It is virtually impossible to remove from clothes, which are best thrown away after a close encounter.

Other mammals are also revolted by it, and so the skunk's only serious predator is the great horned owl, which probably has little need of a sense of smell. Skunks prefer not to waste their musk, as the glands take a couple of days to refill, and so they usually raise their black-and-white tail as a warning before spraying. But such warnings go unheeded on roads, which is why cars are now their worst enemy.

Smelliest animal

NAME	**striped skunk** *Mephitis mephitis*
LOCATION	North America
ABILITY	defending itself with a spray containing the smells that mammals hate most

This is an eel-like animal, 0.5–1m long (20–33 in), without fins, jaws, scales, a backbone or much in the way of eyes. Though not a true fish, it does have gills and excels in a fish-like trait – producing slime. For fish, a thin slime coating is a way of regulating the salt and gas balance between their bodies and the water, repelling parasites and maintaining speed. But for a hagfish, slime is also a weapon.

Its lifestyle is pretty basic, even a little squalid: it lives on the sea-bottom, usually at around 1,200m (4,000ft), where it eats anything it can overcome or scavenge. When it finds a suitable victim, it slithers into it, usually by way of its mouth, and then uses its toothed tongue to rip the animal to pieces from the inside out.

That's nothing, however, compared to what it does when it's threatened. Glands all along its sides exude a slime concentrate that reacts with seawater to create a cloud of mucus goo hundreds of times larger than the original secretions. It's very tough goo, too – reinforced by thousands of long, thin, strong fibres – and the offending predator or unlucky passer-by becomes stuck in it and suffocates. The hagfish itself would suffer a similar fate, except that it has a way of extricating itself: it ties itself into a knot and slips the knot down the length of its body, squeezing free in the process.

Slimiest animal

NAME **hagfish** *Myxini* species
LOCATION worldwide
ABILITY drenching predators in mucus by the bucketful

Keenest hearing

To hunt and orient oneself in the dark requires an extreme sense. Bats do it by 'seeing' with echolocation. They emit high-frequency (ultrasound) pulses from their mouths or noses and analyse the returning echoes to determine the size, shape, texture, location and movements of the smallest of objects. A bat's nose structure helps focus the sound, and its complex ear folds catch the returning echoes. Echoes from above hit the folds at different points to those from below. And by moving its ears, a bat can hear sound bouncing back from different angles.

The noise is so intense that, to avoid going deaf, most bats 'shut off' the sound in their ears as they signal. A bat may 'shout' – at 110 decibels, in the case of the little brown bat, which hunts in open spaces; or it may 'whisper' at 60 decibels, in the case of the northern long-eared bat, which catches insects around vegetation. Bats using lower frequencies (longer wavelengths), such as the greater horseshoe, tend to glean insects off vegetation or hunt large ones; those using higher frequencies (shorter wavelengths) generally catch flying insects at closer range.

While it is difficult to be certain that the greater horseshoe bat has better hearing than other bats, its echolocation system is one of the few studied in detail and it is undoubtedly impressive. But many other bats have incredibly keen hearing, too, and it is possible that the real record-holder has yet to be discovered.

NAME	**greater horseshoe bat**
	Rhinolophus ferrumequinum
LOCATION	Europe and Morocco east to Afghanistan and Japan
ABILITY	tracking and catching insects at speed in total darkness

Stickiest spitter

The spitting spiders are most closely related to the venomous brown recluse spiders. Like the brown recluses, they have only six eyes (as opposed to eight) and relatively poor vision. But they make up for it with their snaring skills. Their main sense is touch and, as the spiders walk, their two front legs, which are longer than the other six, tap the ground ahead, feeling for something edible.

NAME	**spitting spider** *Scytodes* species
LOCATION	worldwide
ABILITY	snaring and immobilising prey with sticky spit

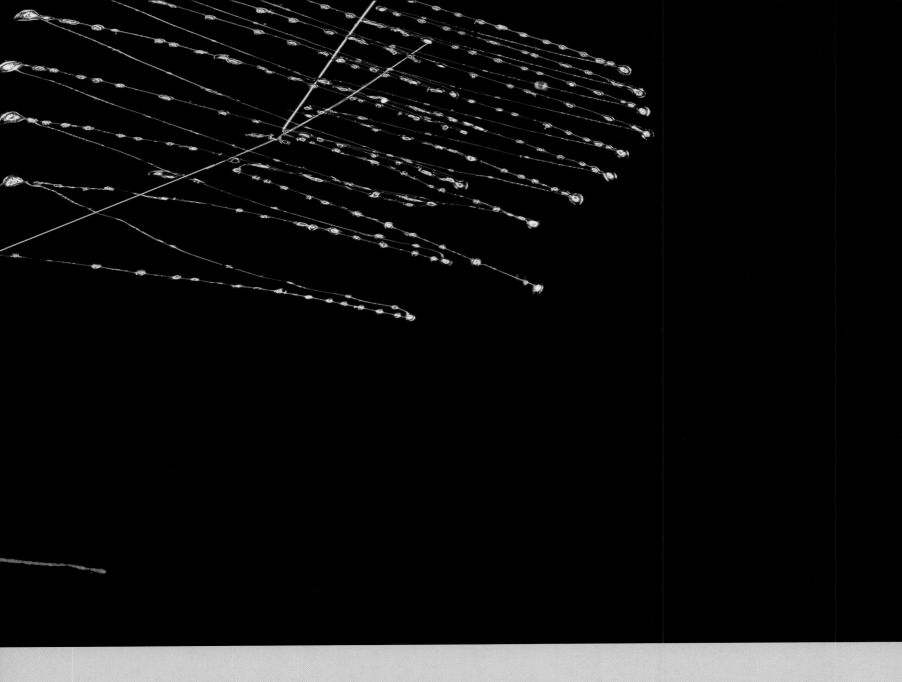

Like all spiders, they lay land lines that they periodically tack down with fast-drying silk, which keep them from falling – just like the ropes of a mountain climber. Many spiders can tell if an insect or another spider crosses these lines, and some spiders are thought to use sensitive hairs on their forelegs to detect something without actually touching it – a form of hearing – while others just feel around. But what all spitting spiders do, once their prey is located, is rear back and spit at it.

With unerring accuracy over a distance that can be more than five times its body length, a spider ejects a gooey mixture of silk and venom. This stuns and immobilises the prey so that the spider can scurry over, bite it to inject more venom and eat it. One probable reason for killing at a distance is that spitting spiders are comparatively small and their jaws don't open wide enough to do more than bite a leg or antenna. The net-like sticky spit also enables them to snare prey that moves faster than they do.

Best colour vision

NAME **stomatopods**, or **mantis shrimps**, in the order Stomatopoda

LOCATION near-shore waters worldwide

ABILITY seeing colours you can't even imagine

A stomatopod's main claim to fame is the power of its spring-loaded, arm-like dactyls: one boxing blow from a 'smasher' stomatopod can punch through the armour of a shellfish. Less famous but probably even more spectacular is their range of colour vision, especially among the stomatopod species that inhabit the clear shallows around kaleidoscopic coral reefs.

The way scientists compare colour vision in different types of animals is by counting the colour photoreceptors in their eyes. Most mammals, for example, have two types. Primates, including humans, do a little better, with three, and most birds and reptiles have four. But stomatopods have at least eight and can detect many colours (including thousands of shades of those) in the ultraviolet wave band – something we can't see at all. A human can discern about 10,000 colours and shades. A stomatopod can see many times that. This is obviously useful around coral reefs, where many creatures use colour as camouflage.

There's also more to their sight than just colour. They have polarisation vision more complex than anything we've been able to create with photography. Their eyes are also on stalks, and can move independently scanning 360 degrees. These are compound eyes with thousands of elements, each of which helps see in depth by perceiving an object from three angles. While we need our entire optical setup for one 'take' in binocular vision, a stomatopod has much more precise, trinocular vision in a single eye.

Most dangerous snake

This all depends on how you measure danger. Whatever is best at killing you is most dangerous. Luckily for humans, no snakes desire to eat us, but some can kill when defending themselves. The one that kills the most often is the saw-scaled viper. The one with the most toxic venom, however, is the sea snake *Hydrophis belcheri.* Like all sea snakes, its venom has evolved to incapacitate fish and suchlike, and it's non-aggressive, lacks the striking fangs of vipers, and bites people only when accidentally handled in fishing nets. More dangerous in terms of fatalities is the beaked sea snake, which inhabits coastal waters and so comes into contact with people more often. Many sea snakes are found in Australian waters, and Australia is also the country with the greatest number of venomous snakes. Eleven of the top 12 most venomous are found here, the world record-holder being the inland taipan, or fierce snake.

But Australia doesn't hold the record for the most dangerous of all land snakes. Taking into account venom toxicity, venom yield, fang length, temperament and frequency of bite, the record goes to the saw-scaled viper. It is widespread, small (therefore easily overlooked) and aggressive when threatened, and it probably bites and kills more people than any other snake. Its name comes from the fact that, when frightened, it rubs its scales together, making a sawing noise – a reminder that most snakes would rather frighten people away than bite them. And, of course, far, far more snakes are killed by people than vice versa.

NAME	**saw-scaled viper** *Echis carinatus*
LOCATION	West Africa through the Middle East to India
ABILITY	injecting a venom that can kill more people than that of any other snake

Extreme

Movement

Strangest hitchhiker · Highest jumper · Largest swarms · Strongest head-butter
Longest non-stop flyer · Most upside-down animal · Most inflatable animal
Heaviest flying animal · Strangest shape-shifter · Fastest flying animal
Greatest sticking power · Largest flying scavenger · Most legs · Speediest sucker
Best long-distance swimmer · Deepest-living animal · Fastest-moving plant
Greatest gathering of birds · Best boring animal · Strongest animal · Best surfer
Earliest-rising songster · Fastest digger · Longest toes · Fastest swimmer
Best water-walker · Fastest long-distance runner · Most elastic tongue
Scariest scamperers · Best glider · Biggest sleep-over · Fastest sprinter
Longest migration · Biggest hunting army · Sleepiest animal

When you are one of nature's midgets, you have to be ingenious to get around. Many tiny arthropods (a group of invertebrates, including insects, crustaceans, spiders and the like) choose to hitch a lift to pastures new. The larva of the California spiny lobster starts life at 3.8cm (1.5in) and spends months travelling in the open ocean, undergoing 11 moults before it gets to be lobster-sized. To escape from predators, it moves down into deeper waters in the day using its long appendages. But to move the hundreds, if not thousands, of kilometres needed to get to its final, adult feeding place, it hitches a lift on a planktonic jellyfish. Making use of the jellyfish's bell-propulsion sailing mechanism means the little lobster no longer has to rely on ocean currents.

Other hitchhikers are more cheeky. The mite *Antennophorus grandis,* for example, chooses to hang on to the underside of the head of a 'nurse' yellow meadow ant, which it matches in size. When it's hungry, it strokes its carrier's head, mimicking a demand for a dollop of regurgitated sugary food that sister ants make on nurses. So it gets free food as well as a place to hang out. The goose barnacle *Alepas pacifica* goes one step further. It hitches a ride with a female jellyfish but snacks all the while on the animal's ovaries. The trouble with being a parasitic freeloader, though, is that you are totally dependent on your chosen host. And if you get too greedy, it could be curtains for both of you.

Strangest hitchhiker

NAME	**larva of the spiny lobster** *Panulirus* species
LOCATION	Pacific Ocean
ABILITY	piggy-back riding

Highest jumper

NAME   **froghopper**, or **leafhopper** species
LOCATION   North America and Eurasia
ABILITY   jumping upwards of 70cm (28in)

The insects thought of as most adapted for a life of jumping are fleas, the champion supposedly being the cat flea, with a jump-height of 24cm (9.6in). Such feats enable them to get to high enough feeding places on moving mammals. But other, less obvious record-beating hoppers easily out-jump them. Froghoppers are plant-sucking bugs capable of flying or jumping to new plants when they need fresh sap. If danger threatens, though, they have an explosive method of escape. The slightest vibration or touch will make these small bugs leap at such speed that a collision with your face would hurt.

The huge 'thigh' muscles controlling their longest hind legs (hidden under their wing cases) are the give-away. Special ridges on these legs (a bit like Velcro) hold them in a permanently cocked position, while the 'thigh' muscles contract slowly, allowing the legs to unlock suddenly and snap open with such force that the bug is catapulted forward. A cuckoospit froghopper accelerates in a millisecond to a take-off velocity of four metres a second, generating a G-force of more than 400 gravities (a human going into orbit in a space rocket will probably experience no more than about five gravities). The force equates to more than 400 times the froghopper's body weight. By comparison, an ordinary flea is way down the scale at 135 times its body weight. But fleas deserve some sort of record, even if it's just for making high jumping into a lifestyle.

Largest swarms

NAME   **desert locust** *Schistocerca gregaria*

LOCATION   northern and eastern Africa, Middle East, south-west Asia

SIZE   billions, covering huge areas

A huge swarm of Rocky Mountain locusts, which were the scourge of western pioneers in North America, once covered a minimum area equivalent in size to England, Scotland, Wales and Ireland combined. As it flew over Nebraska, on 15-25 August 1875, it contained an estimated 25-50 million tonnes (24.6-49.2 million tons) of locusts. Mysteriously, the species became extinct in 1902.

These days, desert locusts form the biggest and most widely destructive insect swarms. One, measured by reconnaissance plane in Kenya in 1954, covered 200sq km (77sq miles). That was only one of several swarms in the same general area, covering a total of about 1,000sq km (386sq miles), reaching an altitude of 1.5 km (0.9 miles) and comprising an estimated 500 billion insects weighing about 100,000 tonnes (98,400 tons).

One of the oddest things about this animal is that it's basically solitary. Most of the time it's a plain, green grasshopper (a locust is essentially a migrating grasshopper). But when the desert conditions change, so do the insects. At times when it's a little wetter than usual and more grasshoppers than usual are hatching out of their underground eggs, they bump into each other – they touch. At this point they're still larvae, known as hoppers because they can't fly yet. But they are already beginning to swarm because the touching releases a 'gregarisation pheromone' (a chemical that makes them gregarious and behave as a group). Masses of them march across the ground in the same direction. This stage lasts about a week, and then they reach maturity and start flying, and the plague begins. There's no specific place where the swarms emerge, but if, say, it's the Arabian Peninsula, the locusts – reproducing as they go – can sweep across Africa, destroying every crop in their path.

Deepest diver

NAME	**sperm whale** *Physeter macrocephalus*
LOCATION	oceans worldwide
ABILITY	diving deeper than any other mammal

Sperm whales behave more like submarines than air-breathing mammals. They disappear into the cold, dark ocean depths to catch deepwater squid or sharks and other large fish.

In 1991, scientists recorded an incredible, record-breaking dive of 2,000m (6,560ft) near the island of Dominica, in the Caribbean. But there is circumstantial evidence to suggest that sperm whales may be able to dive even deeper. On 25 August 1969, for example, a male sperm whale was killed by whalers 160km (100 miles) south of Durban, South Africa. Inside its stomach were two small sharks, which are known to live only on the seafloor. Since the water in that area exceeds a depth of 3,193m (10,475ft) for a radius of some 48-64km (30-40 miles), it is logical to assume that the sperm whale had been to a similar depth when hunting its prey.

The same whale also made one of the longest recorded dives for any mammal. By the time it surfaced to breathe, having caught the two small sharks, it had been underwater for an estimated 1 hour 52 minutes.

Longest non-stop flyer

Depending on how you look at it, several birds could qualify for this record. The Arctic tern, for instance (see p.152), makes the longest migration – at least 30,000 km (18,600 miles) on a yearly round-trip between the Arctic and the Antarctic (and that's only if it goes in a straight line, which it doesn't). Or the wandering albatross (see p.180), which has been radio-tracked on a flight of 15,000km (9,320 miles) lasting 33 days. There's also the tiny rufous hummingbird, just 10cm (3.25in) long, which makes one of the longest trips relative to size – an annual 7,000 km (4,340 miles) and back between Alaska and Mexico.

But the point about swifts is that, except when they're at their nests, they tend just to keep flying. And the reason is quite simple: they have to. A swift's legs are so stumpy that it can't easily perch – and usually doesn't bother. If it ever found itself on the ground, it wouldn't have the leverage to take off again. So a swift can eat, bathe, drink, mate and even sleep on the wing, and from August, when it leaves its nest in Europe or Asia to fly south, it doesn't necessarily stop flying until it returns in April.

More importantly, in its first year of life it doesn't come north to nest, which means that it spends practically two years in the air and flies nearly the distance to the moon and back. Swifts are very busy birds, too. When feeding their chicks, they can make 40 trips a day to the nest, sometimes flying a total of 1,000 km (620 miles).

NAME	**Eurasian swift** *Apus apus*
LOCATION	Europe and Asia, Middle East, north-west Africa, sub-Saharan Africa
LENGTH	500,000 km (310,700 miles)

Unlike most of its relatives, the blue sea slug is blind and spends its life floating upside-down at the surface of the sea, a raft of finger-like projections splayed out and air in its stomach for buoyancy. Passive though it appears, it carries deadly defences – stinging cells – and has predatory intentions. Its beauty is also a disguise: a metallic-sea-blue, upward-facing underside prevents it being seen by birds looking down, and a silvery-white, downward-facing upside camouflages it against fish looking up.

Sooner or later, it will find itself drawn into an eddy, whirlpool, windrow or upwelling aggregation of other animals, where it has a chance of bumping into prey. Its favourite food is both large and armed: the Portuguese man-o'-war (a colony of polyps) and its smaller, single-polyp floating cousins, the by-the-wind-sailor and the blue button. The moment the blue sea slug touches one, it starts to rasp and suck its way through the animal's soft tissues. Somehow, it eats the tentacles and recycles their stinging nematocysts without firing them off, incorporating them for defence into its own finger-like extensions. Should it bump into an anemone attached to floating seaweed, it will dislodge it by grabbing the animal's holdfast and spinning around.

The only other time it abandons its upside-down position is during sex. It's a hermaphrodite, and when a mating couple exchange sperm, they roll around, caressing each other in an embrace that, by comparison with other, more normally orientated animals, is one of the most sensual in the sea.

Most upside-down animal

NAME   **blue sea slug** *Glaucus atlanticus*
LOCATION   mainly sub-tropical and tropical oceans
ABILITY   drifting through life the wrong side up

Most inflatable animal

NAME **pufferfish** *Diodon holocanthus*

LOCATION tropical coastal seas worldwide

ABILITY transforming itself into a spine-covered 'balloon'

This could also be the creature with the greatest number of common names. In English alone, these include spiny puffer, porcupinefish, balloon porcupinefish, brown porcupinefish, blotched porcupinefish, freckled porcupinefish, longspring porcupinefish, hedgehogfish and balloonfish – all of which refer to its defensive quills, its ability to expand, or both. When relaxed, the pufferfish looks pretty ordinary. But if it's attacked, it can suddenly blow itself up to become a spine-covered sphere three times its original size, like a basketball with hundreds of long, thin nails sticking out of it. It does this by taking many rapid gulps of water.

Its stomach, which in the course of evolution has come to be used for nothing else (food is not digested there but passed straight to the intestine), is folded in pleats when the fish isn't puffed up. In fact, there are pleats within pleats within pleats – right down to pleats that can only be seen with a microscope.

When the fish perceives danger, it pumps in water, the stomach unfolds, the skin expands, and the scales – which ordinarily lie backwards against the skin – spring up as spines. As well as dispensing with the normal function of its stomach, the pufferfish has lost most of its skeleton except its backbone (ribs, in particular, would obviously interfere with expansion). A similar sort of oral pumping can also be used offensively: the pufferfish's close relative, the triggerfish, sucks in water and then shoots it out again at sea urchins, flipping them over to reveal their soft undersides.

Heaviest flying animal

NAME   **kori bustard** *Ardeotis kori*

LOCATION   eastern and southern Africa

WEIGHT   possibly more than 22kg (49lb)

Birds range in weight from the 1.6-1.9g (0.06-0.07oz) bee hummingbird to the 150-160kg (332-353lb) ostrich (see p.196), and the main difference between the two extremes is that the hummingbird can fly and the ostrich can't. Even if it had proper wings, the ostrich would be too heavy to fly.

Aerodynamic limitations involving relative size and strength of muscles, body mass, lift, thrust and so on give a weight limit on the possibility of an animal taking to the air, let alone using flapping flight. The largest known bird that ever flew was the 80kg (177lb) extinct giant teratorn (p.111). Some modern flying birds, though, approach the limit for flapping flight. Swans, wild turkeys, wandering albatrosses and Andean condors weigh in the region of 11-15kg (24-35lb). But the record-holder is the kori bustard – and it's not unusual for a male (females are lighter) to weigh 17-19kg (38-42lb).

After a slow and strenuous-looking take-off, a male bustard can fly, but it seems to prefer not to and spends most of its life walking. Flight is reserved mainly for escaping (though the bustard may first attempt to run away) and for local, nomadic migration. But in the case of the excessively heavy and fat individuals (the verified record is 22kg), it seems unlikely that they can actually fly, certainly for any sustained time. There is, of course, a reason for a male bustard choosing to put bulk above flight: height and visibility on the vast African plains are vital for attracting a mate.

Strangest shape-shifter

NAME **cellular slime mould**
Dictyostelium discoideum

LOCATION soil, North America;
biologists' laboratories, worldwide

ABILITY changing from a single cell into a
community slug

This single-celled microbe, affectionately known as Dicty, lives a simple, amoeba-like life in soil and leaf litter, hunting down bacteria. It doesn't bother with sex but creates clones of itself when times are good. But if food gets scarce or it gets too dry, something strange happens. Dicty secretes a hormone that summons others of its kind, including its clones, to form a much larger, single entity.

Up to 100,000 of these microbes converge and form a sort of slug – effectively, a society of individuals covered in a slime sheath. The front-end animals scan ahead and release waves of hormone to keep the 2–3mm (0.1in) stream of individuals moving in the same direction towards the light. Once in the air, the 'pseudoplasmodium' sits up. Individuals then choose different roles. The front-end ones squeeze back down through the rest, anchor, secrete cellulose to form a rigid stem and die.

Meanwhile, the others (70 per cent of the whole) are lifted up or stream up the stem. At the tip they form a ball, each secreting a weather-resistant cellulose coat and transforming into a spore. The spores are dispersed by the wind, and if conditions are right, they 'hatch' back into single-celled microbes. One question that has puzzled scientists is what prompts individuals to opt for a stalk death and sacrifice themselves for the good of the rest, some of which will be unrelated. They may be chemically tricked into doing so, but they can resist such manipulation. So it would seem that there is give and take, even in the world of slime.

The fastest bird (and, indeed, the fastest-moving wild animal of any kind) is certainly a bird of prey and very probably the peregrine falcon. When 'stooping', or plunge-diving, to catch a bird in mid-air, a peregrine weighing just over 1kg (2.2lb) could, theoretically, reach a maximum velocity of 385kph (239mph) in a 1,254m (4,113ft) free-fall. Though there is a difference between how fast it could fly and how fast it actually does fly, a peregrine diving with a skydiver has been filmed at stooping speeds exceeding 322kph (200mph), which is exceedingly close to the theoretical maximum.

What's strange about a peregrine's plunge-dive, though, is that, when the bird is within 1.8km (1.1 miles) of prey, it will fly in a curved path. Biologists now think they know why. A peregrine's vision is such that it sees best when its head is 40 degrees to one side, but to angle its head like this at high speed would cause drag. It is therefore faster for a peregrine to dive on a curve because it can hold its head straight while still keeping its prey in view.

But such flight is not conventional flapping flight. The wandering albatross currently holds the record for the fastest sustained flight, with one individual achieving 56kph (35mph) sustained over more than 800km (497 miles). Albatrosses, though, use 'dynamic soaring', harnessing the power of the wind to glide rather than flapping continuously.

Fastest flying animal

NAME	**peregrine falcon** *Falco peregrinus*
LOCATION	every continent except Antarctica
SPEED	can be more than 300kph (186mph) when plunge-diving

Greatest sticking power

NAME **geckos** Gekkonidae family
LOCATION continent-wide, except Antarctica
ABILITY clinging on to any surface

Most people would think that geckos hang from the ceiling, or any other surface, by suction or perhaps with the help of claws and adhesive. But their sticking power is far more remarkable.

Each foot is covered with half a million microscopic little filaments, called setae, from each of which sprout more than a thousand cauliflower-like fibres, known as spatulae. When these spatulae splay, they are so close to the surface that a tiny charge is generated between their molecules and those of the surface, which draws them to each other, the positive pole of one attracting the negative pole of the other. This is enhanced by the geckos' mechanism of toe uncurling, which enables them to attach and peel off their feet 15 times a second while running. The molecular force is so strong that a foot on glass, with its millions of spatulae all generating molecular force, could support 40kg (88lb).

This mechanism also includes a self-cleaning component: any dirt attached to the setae falls off after just a few steps, the attractive forces between the dirt and the setae being less than those between the surface and the dirt. The geckos' cling-on capacity is inspiring technologists to develop everything from a self-cleaning, easily detachable adhesive tape to sure-footed micro-robots for use in space. Jumping spiders, though, almost certainly got there first, being able to support up to 170 times their own weight using the same molecular mechanism.

Largest flying scavenger

NAME   **Andean condor** *Vultur gryphus*

LOCATION   Andes, South America

SIZE   a wingspan up to 3.2m (10ft 5in), 8–15kg (18–33lb)

Condors are scavengers – vultures – rather than birds of prey. Though they do occasionally catch seabirds, they are not designed for speed or stealth. Instead, they spend much of their time gliding around in search of dead animals. And the master glider is the largest of them all – the Andean condor. It's perfectly designed for such a lifestyle: its feet are used as air breaks and for walking and grasping rather than grabbing and killing; its head and neck are relatively feather-free, enabling it to reach into a carcass without messing up its plumage; its large bill is sharp for slicing hide; and it has strong masticating muscles, enabling it to tear off large chunks of meat.

Nonetheless, there is one drawback to the design. The Andean condor can't run well, and with such huge wings, is too heavy and cumbersome to get airborne easily by flapping. So it must live where there are strong updrafts and thermals to assist take-off. Once airborne, though, a condor can soar effortlessly, and its primary feathers act as aerofoils, enabling precision turns as it scans for food below. It hasn't got a good sense of smell, but it follows those vultures that can sniff out carcasses, and its huge size means that it is top of the pecking order when it arrives.

In prehistoric times, there existed a South American glider that was twice the size of a condor: the teratorn, the largest-ever flying bird. But this was no scavenger. Its beak could open wide enough to engulf hare-sized prey whole – making it probably the scariest bird ever to have lived.

Though 'milli' means a thousand and 'pede' means foot, no millipede has a thousand feet. Unlike centipedes, which have one pair of legs to a segment, millipedes appear to have two. But each millipede segment is, in fact, two segments fused together – a clever way of cutting down on bulk while building up legs. Though it's born with only a few segments, a millipede adds more – and therefore more legs – at every moult. Such a huge number of short, muscular legs gives lift and pushing power, making millipedes slow but strong, unlike the predatory centipedes, which are flat, low to the ground and fast movers. Most millipedes are also cylindrical and bulldozer-like and burrow for decaying plant matter (making them valuable forest recyclers), preferring to roll up rather than run from danger.

Each pair of legs moves slightly out of phase with the pairs in front and behind, resulting in a wave-like movement of legs along the body. A female millipede finds the rhythmic tapping of hundreds of legs sweeping along her body very sexy, and so the male caresses her as a prelude to mating. He also has a pair of 'sex legs', or gonopods, for transferring his package of sperm to her genital opening. Having many legs is handy for cleaning, and most millipedes are fastidious about cleanliness, spending much of their free time scrubbing and polishing, even using one pair of legs as brushes for their antennae.

Most legs

NAME **Millipede**

LOCATION worldwide

NUMBER up to 750 legs in 375 pairs

A smallish fish spots an even smaller one swimming enticingly slowly towards an innocuous stone. As it darts in the little fish's direction, it feels a whoosh of suction, everything goes black, and that's the last thing it knows. It's been frogfished.

There are 43 species of frogfish, with different colours (and the ability to change colour to match their surroundings), different sizes and different disguises: some look like sponges, some like encrusted stones, some like clumps of seaweed, some like very unfishlike blobs simply hanging in the water. But what they have in common is the ability to look like inanimate and other animate objects. They also have a dorsal fin that has evolved into a fishing pole, complete with line and artificial lure – which can 'wiggle' like a fish, a worm or a shrimp – and a mouth that can open cavernously wide, suck like the front end of a jet engine and shut again, all in one sixth of a second.

Frogfish can also be, in their various and ingenious means of disguise, monstrously ugly. But they didn't evolve to please the sensibilities of humans. What they did turn out to be were animals with the ability to extend their mouths and engulf their victims faster than any other vertebrate predator. (How fast and exactly what they do wasn't even discovered until the invention of high-speed cinematography.) Frogfish are among the few predators capable of wholly swallowing animals that are larger than themselves. And they are also among the planet's greatest masters of disguise.

Speediest sucker

NAME	**frogfish** *Antennarius* species
LOCATION	coral reefs worldwide
ABILITY	instantly changing from a stone to a vacuum sucker

The annual round-trip of grey whales is not only an impressive feat of long-distance swimming but is also probably the longest regular migration of any population of mammals. Migration takes place between their summer feeding grounds west and north of Alaska and their winter breeding grounds in a series of shallow lagoons along Mexico's Baja California. The greys commute along the entire length of the North American coastline, and back again, every year.

There's one other whale, though, that muddies this claim a little – the humpback (see p.32). Humpbacks are mighty migrators, too, though not quite on the scale of the greys, travelling between cool-water feeding grounds and warm-water breeding grounds in both the Atlantic and the Pacific. They do, though, hold the record for the longest confirmed migration by any individual mammal. In 1990, a humpback seen off the Antarctic Peninsula was spotted five months later off Colombia (the whales are individually recognisable by the black and white markings on the undersides of their tail flukes), an impressive journey of 8,330km (5,175 miles) or a 16,660km (10,350 miles) round-trip.

Since then, several other humpbacks have been identified in both places – which confirms that the first one wasn't merely lost. But it's not necessarily a record-breaking migration on the scale of the entire population of the eastern North Pacific grey whales. Anyway, the grey holds one even prouder distinction: the most impressive recovery by a great whale. In the late 1930s, when greys were officially protected, there were only a few hundred left. Now there are estimated to be a healthy 26,000.

Best long-distance swimmer

NAME **grey whale** *Eschrichtius robustus*

LOCATION North Pacific Ocean

ABILITY swimming up to 16,000km (9,900 miles) a year

Deepest-living animal

NAME **amphipod** *Hirondellea gigas*
LOCATION Mariana Trench, Pacific Ocean
ABILITY thriving 11 km (6.8 miles) below sea level at a pressure of 1,000 atmospheres

In 1995, using the only remotely operated vehicle that could withstand pressures 1,000 times greater than the pressure at sea level, scientists finally probed the deepest place on Earth. They explored the Challenger Deep region of the Mariana Trench in the Pacific Ocean, 11,000m (36,000ft) below sea level – deeper than Mount Everest is high – and they found bacteria. In particular, they found a cream-coloured, sausage-shaped colony of a species later called *Moritella yayanosii*, whose ability to survive such extreme conditions, using special enzymes and proteins, offers the promise of medical breakthroughs.

But they also found amphipods – lots of them. Amphipods are diverse crustaceans that include sandhoppers, and which live on the seafloor from the poles to the equator. But one big hopper, at 4.5cm (1.8in), was scampering around in one of the most hostile environments on Earth, in absolute darkness, where there is little food and under a pressure that would kill most other animals.

Hirondellea gigas has only been found in the very-deep sea. It has a slow metabolism and a large gut but can swim surprisingly fast. It survives by scavenging on falls of 'marine snow' – the remains of animals that slowly sink to the depths – and must either be plentiful or have a remarkable sense of smell, as when bait is laid down, it invariably turns up. With technology allowing more deep-sea voyages, the likelihood is that more communities of 'extreme' animals will be found living at such depths.

Fastest-moving plant

NAME **Venus flytrap** *Dionaea muscipula*
LOCATION bogs in North and South Carolina
ABILITY grabbing insects at a speed of a fraction of a second

Plants may have limitations on movement, and they don't have muscle power, but there are ways round that. The Venus flytrap uses elasticity to set its two-lobed, snap-jaw trap. The animals it kills provide the nitrogen and other essential minerals it needs to stay healthy and set seed in its nutrient-poor, water-logged and acidic habitat.

The upper side of each lobe is stretched tauter than the underside (its cells elongate under water pressure) and the lobe curves back by tension, like a bow. It lures insects with nectar, which it produces via glands along the rims of the lobes. The trap is released when several of the six or so sensitive trigger hairs sense movement and send chemical-electric signals that cause water transfer between cells, releasing the tension. The result is an instantaneous shutting of the trap.

The Venus flytrap is also to be admired for another talent. It can 'decide' if something inanimate is in the trap, by counting whether there are two or more stimulations of the hairs – any fewer and the trap won't work. The lobes tighten to form a seal as enzymes are released (with antiseptic to deter bacteria and fungi) and then the prey is digested. A week or so later, the trap is ready to kill again.

Only bladderworts rival the flytrap for speed. They catch tiny creatures under water with bladder traps, closing the seals of their traps in a similarly tiny fraction of a second.

Greatest gathering of birds

NAME **Red-billed quelea** *Quelea quelea*
LOCATION eastern and southern Africa
SIZE 30 million or more together

The North American passenger pigeon is widely believed to have been the commonest bird that has ever lived on Earth. It lived in huge, densely packed flocks (some containing more than 2,000 million individuals), which darkened the sky and could take up to three days to pass overhead. But the species was hunted to extinction in less than 100 years and the last individual died on 1 September 1914.

Today, it is queleas that gather in the world's largest flocks. They're also, as far as anybody can tell, the world's most numerous bird. The population is so large it is effectively uncountable – though usually guessed to be in the hundreds of millions. Put it this way: there are so many queleas that every year southern Africans can kill 65–180 million of them without appearing to make a dent in the overall population size. And the reason so many people are so anxious to kill these rather pretty sparrow-sized finches (apart from putting them in the pot) has to do with those greatest bird gatherings.

Queleas are agricultural pests, often called 'feathered locusts'. When they swarm, they eat, and among the things they eat are cereal crops if there are any around – millet, sorghum, wheat and rice – and in a short time they can wipe out an entire harvest. The natural food of queleas is wild grass seed, which, as migrants, they find by following the rains. Once they've located a good supply, all the birds from hundreds of kilometres around gather there, turning trees into masses of feathers and even breaking branches with their combined weight. They will also feed on insects, especially when raising chicks, and this actually helps local farmers by clearing out their other crop pests. This should, of course, put agricultural people in two minds about queleas. But while most never appreciate the pest-control role, some are mindful that, when swarms of queleas appear, it's time for a delicious feast.

A caecilian looks like a cartoon of an earthworm. The blunt head resembles the tail, but with jaws and sharp teeth, and the body is divided into glistening segments. Caecilians do have a connection with earthworms – many species eat little else – but they are vertebrates (have backbones) and are in fact related to newts and salamanders. They have, though, lost their legs, can hardly see and have very little to do with water. They range from a worm-sized 7cm (2.7in) to an improbable 1.5m (4.9ft) and are practically never seen by people because most live a subterranean existence.

Caecilians are remarkably good at boring through the ground. Most elongated tunnelling animals, such as worms and snakes, use what's called a normal concertina movement – going from a closed concertina to an open one, as the tail muscles push the head and upper body forward. The caecilian, however, always keeps its body straight.

It also appears to go through the ground like a self-propelled iron rod, hammering the sometimes very hard earth aside with its head (not that you could ever watch it underground, but scientists in laboratories put caecilians into clear, dirt-filled plastic tubes). In fact, it is using an internal concertina movement. Its vertebral column is flexing and extending, just as a snake's would, but the skeleton isn't connected to the outer sheath of skin. As the skeleton moves, the outer part of the caecilian stays straight, rippling along and giving the animal traction, somewhat like the treads on a tank.

Best boring animal

NAME   **caecilian** species
LOCATION tropical regions
ABILITY   hammering its way through hard ground

Rhinoceros beetles belong to the scarab family, many of which are so incredibly strong that they can do things like roll huge dung balls or bury other animals. But the rhinoceros beetle is supposedly the strongest: one laboratory animal reputedly lifted a weight on its back 850 times its own weight, far exceeding the relative strength of an elephant.

Even if the record is exaggerated, there is no doubt about the beetle's strength. Males are famous for their forked 'horns': an enormous one arching over the head and a smaller one arching up to meet it. When females are ready to mate (they spend most of the time below ground, feeding on plant material and possibly keeping out of the way of males), they waft out an attractive pheromone scent that brings males flying in. This is when the horns clash. The biggest beetles – heaviest and longest – are those that have fed on the best food and so, possibly, have the best potential to father offspring. But they must prove themselves to onlooking females. Duelling males first threaten each other with head bobbing. Then the head-butting, levering and tossing starts, the loser finally being prised off his perch. The bigger a male is, the bigger his horns, the stronger his muscles and gripping legs, and the more likely he is to win. But bigger isn't always better. In the case of some horned scarab beetles, males that have invested in huge horns turn out to have small genitalia.

Strongest animal

NAME **rhinoceros beetle** *Xylotrupes gideon*
LOCATION Asia
ABILITY lifting possibly up to 850 times its own weight

Best surfer

Bottlenose dolphins are highly social mammals, usually travelling in pods of 2–15 individuals and, offshore, in herds of tens or even hundreds. They often hunt cooperatively and, like many social predators, are inquisitive and adventurous. They frequently investigate people in the water, play with flotsam and jetsam and with other animals such as sea urchins and with seaweed (throwing these 'toys' around seemingly for fun) and will go out of their way to ride in the bow-waves in front of boats and ships.

It's hard not to be anthropomorphic, because they seem to take pleasure in these apparently frivolous activities and seldom do them for any obvious practical reason. Bow-riding, for example, is often a distraction from feeding or from travelling in a different direction. So perhaps it is inevitable that they should enjoy surfing. Common bottlenose dolphins and their close relatives Pacific bottlenose dolphins, which are found in the western North Pacific and around the Indian Ocean, can be seen body-surfing huge breakers close to shore. Sometimes they are in the company of human surfers, racing in towards the beach and then swimming back through the surf and spray to wait for the next big wave. Given their other games and antics, it is almost impossible to come up with an explanation for the activity other than that they do it for the sheer thrill of the ride, just as we do.

NAME	**common bottlenose dolphin**
	Tursiops truncatus
LOCATION	temperate and tropical waters worldwide
ABILITY	surfing and 'bow-riding' – probably just for fun

Earliest-rising songster

Birdwatchers have long known that the thrush family – particularly the robin, blackbird, song thrush and American robin – are among the earliest daytime songsters. In UK surveys of early avian choristers, robins and blackbirds inevitably come top, with the robin winning overall. Robins are also more likely to sing at night, when they are sometimes stimulated by streetlights, though night singing can be dangerous if owls or other predators are about. Males tend to do most of the singing: a male robin sings to defend his territory and to attract a mate. His singing decreases once he has a suitable partner, but he continues a certain amount of singing to keep her and to arouse her for mating prior to egg-laying.

Dawn is the time when weather conditions most favour song transmission, but weather is not the key factor in encouraging song. It's a combination of daylight and male hormones. As daylight lengthens during spring and early summer, there is a decrease in the production of melatonin (produced in the brain at night) and this triggers an enlargement of the song area of the brain.

Early songsters tend to have (proportionately) larger eyes than later-rising songsters. This helps them to see better in low light: they usually start feeding earlier and can keep watch for predators. The male robin spends most of the day foraging and, if energy levels are sufficiently high, sings a little bit in the evening. But he tries to keep enough energy in reserve, after a relatively short night's sleep, to serenade full pelt once again as the day dawns.

NAME	**European robin** *Erithacus rubecula*
LOCATION	Europe, south to North Africa, east to Siberia
ABILITY	singing before dawn, often earlier than any other bird

The aardvark is one of the world's strangest mammals. It has no close relatives alive today, though distant ones include elephants, manatees and golden moles, and no animals behave quite like it. Aardvark is Dutch for 'earth pig' and, being plump and hairless, it makes a juicy meal. A nocturnal lifestyle, combined with a good sense of smell and radar-like ears, helps it to evade some predators.

But its chief means of defence is burrowing. It has long, chisel-like claws at the end of enormously powerful, muscular legs, and these make it possibly the fastest-burrowing animal in the world. Reputedly, it can dig a burrow in soft earth faster than two men with spades. The burrows it digs as daytime sleeping dens also act as bolt-holes and are long enough – often more than 10m (33ft) or so – to dissuade a predator such as a hyaena from trying to dig out the aardvark or its babies.

The claws are also designed for digging termites and ants out of hard-baked earth. In fact, the aardvark's whole body is devised for anting. At night, it zig-zags across the savannah with its snout down, and as soon as it detects a termite nest, it starts digging. Nose hairs filter out dust, and its 45cm (17in) long, saliva-wet tongue extracts termites and ants at speed. Its termite-grinding teeth grow continuously but lack roots or enamel. A life of digging and dirt seems to work, though, as aardvarks are found in most parts of Africa where ants and termites abound.

Fastest digger

NAME	**aardvark** *Orycteropus afer*
LOCATION	African savannah, grassland and open woodland
ABILITY	digging for a living

Longest toes

NAME **northern jacana** *Jacana spinosa*

LOCATION Mexico and Central America

SIZE 14cm (5.5in) – the longest toes relative to body length

The northern jacana (one of eight jacana species found in the tropics around the world) is 23cm (9in) tall and has an astonishing toe-span – 11.5cm (4.5in) wide and 14cm (5.5in) long. That would be like a 1.8m (6ft) man having feet 0.9m (3ft) wide and 1.1m (3.6ft) long.

The jacana is sometimes called 'the Jesus Christ bird' because of its apparent ability to walk on water. It can't quite do that, of course, but it can walk on floating vegetation – broad stands of water hyacinth, water lilies, water lettuce – by spreading its weight across a wide area. This is where it spends most of its life, free of competition from birds and mammals that don't have such special feet.

The other distinction the jacana is known for is its sexual 'role reversal'. A female usually has four mates, all occupying different territories. When it's time to breed, she copulates with all of them, again and again and in rapid succession, and when she lays her eggs – a clutch of four, normally – she leaves them with one of the males and rushes off to mate again. Even though there's only one chance in four that any particular chick will be his, the male left with the eggs dutifully incubates them and, when the chicks hatch, he looks after them. He defends them, too, dashing back and forth on his pontoon feet at any sign of a threat.

Fastest swimmer

NAME **sailfish** *Istiophorus platypterus*

LOCATION warm waters worldwide

SPEED up to 109kph (68mph)

It is notoriously difficult to measure the speed of a fish, and as no one has yet set up an open-water fish-racing track, we must rely on fishermen's estimates. The sailfish's predatory behaviour and its body structure indicate a good turn of speed. Like the nose of a jet, its rapier-like bill has been shown to cause what's called 'low-resistance flow'. And it is undoubtedly fast, recorded as reeling out 91m (300ft) of a fisherman's line in 3 seconds – faster than a sprinting cheetah (though estimates based on charging leaps out of water aren't necessarily the same as top *swimming* speed).

Close behind the sailfish in the speed-ratings are other open-water hunters: in order, swordfish, marlin, wahoo, yellowfin tuna and bluefin tuna. One of the secrets of the sailfish's speed, along with that of these other fast predators, lies in its musculature. It has huge amounts of white muscle (great for acceleration but not stamina), boosted along the flanks by blocks of red muscle (needing more oxygen but good for sustained fast swimming). Most of the heat produced by the red muscle fibres is retained by a special network of blood vessels, making the blood warmer than the surrounding water. It can also channel warm blood to the brain and eyes, helping it to spot and chase prey in colder water and at depth.

The exact function of its huge dorsal fin, the 'sail', remains to be discovered, but it is thought to assist in fast-turning manoeuvres, increase the fish's profile when it's rounding up prey, act as a sail when the fish is at the surface and warm the blood when it is exposed to the sun.

'Water skater' is a more appropriate name than 'water strider' for this remarkable insect, as it uses the surface tension of still water, such as on ponds, almost as though it were a layer of thin ice. Surface tension is not something that big, heavy animals notice much, but what happens is this: below the surface, molecules of water are attracted towards other molecules of water in all directions – up, down and sideways. At the surface, though, the molecules cannot go further upwards, and so it's all sideways and down. This creates what amounts to a physical film firm enough to support something very light.

The skater's long legs also have microscopic hairs that trap air and make the legs more hydrophobic, or water-repellent, and the more hydrophobic something is, the heavier it can be and still be supported by the surface tension. The skater's legs don't get wet at all. As the insect moves across the water at speeds of up to 75cm (30in) a second, it makes little indentations, or dimples, in the surface tension and then uses the dimples as though they were the blades of oars – in fact, it rows across the water. And it only runs (or rows) on four of its six legs. The front two are very short and sensitive. They can tell when something breaks the surface, and if that something is small and keeps moving, the strider will dart over, grab it and eat it.

Best water-walker

NAME	**water skater**, or **water strider**, *Gerris* species
LOCATION	tropical and temperate zones worldwide
ABILITY	walking on water as if it were dry ground

Fastest long-distance runner

NAME **pronghorn** *Antilocapra americana*

LOCATION plains of western North America and northern Mexico

SPEED up to 88.5kph (55mph) for 0.8km (0.5 miles)

The pronghorn is seriously unique. It is neither an antelope nor a deer but is in a family of its own. It is built for both speed and endurance and, though the cheetah holds the speed record and can run faster, no other animal can run so fast over a sustained distance. The pronghorn has, for example, been recorded cruising at 67kph (42mph) for 1.6 km (1 mile), which would get it a speeding ticket in a built-up area.

But why such speed? Scientists believe that, in prehistoric times, it was probably hunted not only by plains wolves, which have stamina, but also by a now-extinct predator with both stamina and speed – probably a super-cheetah. And, of course, there is nowhere to hide on the wide-open prairies.

Recent research has also revealed some of the pronghorn's physiological secrets. For a start, it has powerful lower-torso muscles and extremely long, lightweight legs. In full gallop, the front legs push right forward and the hind legs back, allowing a long, airborne stride. Compared to most other mammals, its heart, lungs and windpipe are larger, and its blood is unusually rich in haemoglobin – which means that more oxygen can be delivered to the muscles in less time. It also has huge, protruding eyes that give wide peripheral vision, for spotting predators on the plains, and binocular vision, critical for speed running. Alas, the pronghorn couldn't outrun the guns of European settlers, who by the early 1900s had reduced its numbers from possibly 40 million to just 10,000–20,000.

Most elastic tongue

At first analysis, a chameleon shouldn't be able to do what it does. It's spectacular enough that in just ten seconds the lizard can become an entirely different colour, but the way it uses its tongue makes even that seem pedestrian.

X-ray film and high-speed video have revealed that a chameleon's tongue on its way to an insect starts relatively slowly but then accelerates to 6m (20ft) a second in just 20 milliseconds. This is a faster acceleration than sheer muscular force could ever manage. Then when the tip of tongue reaches the target, which can be more than two of the chameleon's body lengths away, it can attach to prey as heavy as 15 per cent of the chameleon's own weight (large ones can grab birds or lizards) and, with nothing on the tongue stickier than viscous saliva, can haul the prey back quickly and easily.

How? First, the shot: it's been discovered that between its tongue bone and tongue muscle a chameleon has some elastic collagen tissue that the muscle stretches before the tongue is released, the same way a bowstring is stretched to shoot an arrow. Second, the grab: there's another muscle at the tip of the tongue that contracts in the instant before the prey is hit, converting the tip from convex to concave and making a powerful suction cup. Third, the retrieval: more tongue muscles and special filaments allow for 'supercontraction', like an accordion slammed shut. And it all happens in a little more than a second.

NAME	**chameleons** Chamaeleonidae family
LOCATION	mainly Africa and Madagascar, but also the Middle East, southern Europe, and Asia
ABILITY	capturing prey with a bowstring, suction-cup, accordion tongue

In the Middle East they run at 40kph (25mph), jump 2m (6ft) in the air and lay their eggs in camels' bellies. They're huge, and what's more they're venomous. In Mexico they're called matevenados – deer-killers – and they're more deadly than scorpions. In South Africa they actually chase people.

Well, none of those stories is actually true, but you only need to see the frenzied way a solifugid searches for and consumes its prey to understand how such tales have arisen. An eight-legged arachnid with a pair of pedipalps (appendages either side of the mouth) that look like two more legs, it eats insects, spiders and scorpions and sometimes stretches to small mammals or reptiles, depending on its size, from a few millimetres to 15cm (6in) long. At night, when most solifugids are active, they zig-zag across the ground at ferocious speed, grabbing anything they come across and then stopping to crunch it with what may be the most powerful jaws, relative to overall size, in the animal kingdom.

Solifugids are insatiable. Towards the end of a good night's hunting, they can be so bloated they can hardly move, but they'll still eat anything they can catch. They're not venomous, though a bite from a large one can draw blood from a human. As for chasing people, it's the rare diurnal ones that gave rise to that story. All they're doing is trying to cool off by staying in a human's shadow – which, nevertheless, must be rather disconcerting.

Scariest scamperers

NAME	**solifugids**, **wind spiders**, **wind scorpions**, or **sun scorpions** Solifugidae family
LOCATION	arid regions worldwide
ABILITY	frantic killing and eating

Best glider

NAME **Japanese giant flying squirrel**
Petaurista leucogenys

LOCATION Japan, Korea and China

ABILITY flying – almost

Flying squirrels don't really fly. They don't have wings that they flap to give themselves thrust. But they do glide. Along with five other classifications of mammal, and certain lizards and snakes, they glide between trees to save energy and to avoid the dangers implicit in scurrying along the ground.

The best of the gliding animals (aside from wind-surfing birds) would be the one whose glide is longest, most agile and comes closest to flight. A typical glider goes near enough in a straight line from the tree it was in to the tree it's aiming for, floating on the out-spread membranes between its fore and hind legs. But the giant flying squirrel is more agile than that. By changing the position of its legs, it can alter its direction and perform impressive fast turns and banks. It can even ride the warm air currents rising from the valleys in its native mountain home, like a soaring bird.

Its close relative, the giant red flying squirrel, is also an outstanding glider and the two species can travel further than any other non-flying glider – more than 110m (361ft). To travel such long distances, and to get up speed, they simply hold their legs close to their bodies and fall. They hurtle towards the ground at a heart-stopping rate and then open their membranes – and glide.

Every August and September, monarch butterflies in North America receive a mysterious message from their genes. They stop their routines, either check the position of the sun or sense the Earth's magnetic field (nobody knows for sure) and start flapping and gliding their way south. By November, they're in the mountains of Central Mexico – millions of them – blanketing groves of fir trees in about 20 different locations. It's the world's most massive insect migration: virtually all the monarchs east of the Rocky Mountains participate.

Once they've settled on their trees, they don't move out again until February or March, when they snap out of their torpor, mate and fly north. As they reach the southern US, the females seek out milkweed plants (nothing else will do) and lay eggs on them. Then all the butterflies die. When the eggs hatch, the caterpillars dine on milkweed, form their chrysalids, hatch and, as new butterflies, head further north. Then two or three generations later (the summer butterfly generations live shorter lives than the overwintering ones), it's August again, and they get the genetic signal to migrate. So instead of becoming sexually mature and mating – as their parents, grandparents and great-grandparents did – the monarchs head for Mexico.

Sadly, recent studies indicate that the numbers of monarch butterflies sleeping for the winter in the fir forests are decreasing. The cause is probably a combination of illegal logging in their Mexican sanctuaries and the use of pesticides to kill milkweed plants in North America, and conservationists are now desperately trying to find ways to safeguard the world's biggest sleep-over.

Biggest sleep-over

NAME **monarch butterfly** *Danaus plexippus*
LOCATION North America
NUMBERS millions overwinter together in Mexico

A cheetah actually spends most of its time resting from the heat, hiding from other big cats or sitting high up looking for prey. But the action, when it happens, is sudden. After stalking its prey as closely as possible, it sprints from almost a standing start. Film of one chase showed the cheetah reaching 80kph (56mph) in just three seconds. But the official record was set by a cheetah in Kenya that clocked an average 103kph (64mph) over 201m (220yds).

At top speed, a cheetah's incredibly flexible spine gives it a stride length relatively twice that of a racehorse's – so long that all four feet are off the ground for more than half the distance. Other design features include tough, gripping pads, non-retractable claws like running-shoe spikes, very long, thin, tendon-spring legs, a rotary gallop that allows it to make sudden changes in direction and a long tail to help balance those moves.

A cheetah doesn't always run at top speed, however, and usually gives up after 60 seconds. The average chase is no further than 200–300m (219–328yds) and no more than 20 seconds, after which the animal, panting frantically, has to rest for at least 20 minutes to cool off and to let the build-up of lactic acid from its super-speed muscles dissipate. Not surprisingly, prey animals such as impalas and gazelles have evolved to run fast, too – a Thomson's gazelle has been recorded at 94.2kph (58.5mph), fast enough to keep any cheetah on its toes.

Fastest sprinter

NAME	**cheetah** *Acinonyx jubatus*
LOCATION	grassland and semi-desert regions of Africa, with possibly a few left in the Middle East and Asia
SPEED	up to 103kph (64mph)

Longest migration

NAME   **Arctic tern**, or **sea swallow**,
Sterna paradisaea

DESTINATIONS   Arctic and Antarctic

LENGTH   30,000 km (18,600 miles) round-trip

One look at the Arctic tern tells you it's an aerodynamic master and ace diver. Its body is slim and streamlined, its tail and wings long and pointed to minimise air resistance, its wings elbowed for plunge-diving and its bill spear-like. Those terns breeding during the northern summer in the high Arctic and 'wintering' during the southern summer in the Antarctic do a round-trip of at least 30,000 km (18,600 miles) measured as a straight line. Many do more, depending on their starting points and weather conditions, preferring to hug the continental coastlines rather than fly cross-country.

The longest distance recorded for any single bird is held by a ringed Arctic tern that left Finland on or about 15 August 1996. After flying via the English Channel and down the west coasts of Europe and Africa, it probably turned east at the Cape of Good Hope and crossed the Indian Ocean to arrive in Victoria, Australia, on 24 January. That's more than 25,760 km (16,000 miles) – about 160 km (100 miles) a day. No doubt it refuelled along the route, as unlike land-based migrants, a tern is designed for sea fishing and can therefore fly offshore for the whole journey without needing to carry extra fuel and weight in the form of fat.

The breeding and wintering destinations are both worth the effort. In the high Arctic, insect numbers are huge, benefiting chicks as well as adults, and fish plentiful; the Antarctic, too, has huge numbers of fish and crustaceans. Both also provide almost perpetual daylight, allowing this high-performance bird non-stop, year-round fishing.

Biggest hunting army

NAME **army ants** and **driver ants** *Eciton* and *Dorylus* species
LOCATION Central and South America (army ants); Africa (driver ants)
ABILITY form raiding parties that may number 500,000 individuals

Many carnivorous animals hunt cooperatively. But driver ants of Africa and army ants of Central and South America, which live in colonies of up to 20 million, are the all-time record-holders. With hundreds of thousands working together on a raid, they actually blur the line between related individuals working together and a single organism with many working parts. But however you look at them, when army or driver ants are on the march, they are formidable.

They move quite slowly, and so larger animals – reptiles or mammals – can usually get out of their way. Though the sheer number of African driver ants, which have cutting 'jaws' and form long, wide columns, sometimes kills chickens and tethered domestic animals. But insects and other invertebrates, such as spiders and scorpions, are not so fortunate. Both army and driver ants sense potential prey mainly by the vibrations as it flees, and both operate using essentially the same division of labour. There's a great mass of workers, protected on their flanks by larger 'soldiers' armed with powerful weapons: army ants have tissue-dissolving stings, and driver ants have powerful bites.

Army ant workers are the front-line raiders that do most of the killing, but soldiers guard them and the captured prey, and are often stationed behind to catch any prey that has escaped the main attack. The booty is dismembered and carried by teams of porters back to the bivouac, the queen's mobile chamber, which is made out of the living bodies of workers and contains the colony's hungry larvae.

A three-toed sloth has two modes of being: not quite asleep and asleep. It can sleep for up to 20 hours a day: the longest lifespan recorded for a sloth is 30 years, which means that that animal spent 25 years asleep. A sloth sleeps hanging upside-down from a tree branch, which is also what it does when it's awake. The difference is that, when it's awake, it pulls leaves off the tree incredibly slowly and eats them incredibly slowly. Then it moves along the branch at a speed that's been worked out at 0.5kph (0.3mph) or less than 14m (45ft) a minute.

On a really eventful day, it descends to the ground and very slowly and awkwardly – since this is the only time it's ever upright – makes its way to the next tree. Sometimes the next tree is on the other side of a river or marsh, in which case the sloth swims to it, using a kind of dog-paddle that's strong and rather graceful compared to its walking but is, of course, very slow.

A sloth's metabolism is much lower than that of other mammals, and in the morning it gets up to speed by sunning itself. It also digests slowly and only defecates once a week: for this event it comes slowly down from its tree, slowly digs a hole and deposits a third of its body weight (including urine) into it. Even the faeces, which are hard and dry, decompose at about a tenth the rate of other animals' faeces.

Sleepiest animal

NAME	**brown-throated three-toed sloth** *Bradypus variegatus*
LOCATION	Central America and tropical South America
ABILITY	doing as little as possible

Extreme

Growth

Longest fangs · Greatest number of teeth · Fastest-growing plant · Smallest fish

Most gargantuan of growths · Heaviest land animal · Oldest living animal

Smallest reptile · Longest whiskers · Oldest surviving fish · Largest wingspan

Most elastic animal · Longest snake · Tallest living thing · Biggest brain

Largest superorganism · Longest tongue · Most numerous animal · Biggest bird

Largest animal ever · Longest weapons · Oldest living clone · Longest hair

Hairiest animal · Biggest mouth · Most feathers · Tallest animal · Most impressive

tooth · Largest eyes · Heaviest living thing · Fattest carnivore · Longest fin

Largest flower · Smallest amphibian · Most elongated fish · Baggiest animal

Oldest leaves · Rarest animal · Tiniest mammal · Oldest surviving seed plant

Largest reptile · Heaviest tree dweller · Flattest animal · Biggest canopy

Longest fangs

NAME **gaboon viper** *Bitis gabonica*
LOCATION West Africa
SIZE up to 5cm (2in) long

With a maximum known length of 2.2m (7.2ft), the gaboon viper is the largest of the three African snakes in the group known as the giant vipers (the other two being the puff adder and the rhinoceros viper). It is one of the world's top-ten most venomous snakes and has the distinction of delivering the highest average yield of venom in a bite (actually, it shares this distinction with the king cobra of southern Asia – the world's longest venomous snake). It typically injects 350–600mg of venom and, since 60mg is considered a fatal dose for a human, a total yield of gaboon viper venom could theoretically kill 6–10 people.

When it comes to the length of its fangs, the viper beats the cobra by no less than 3.5cm (1.5in). This, of course, means that the gaboon viper bites deeper than any other venomous snake. Why it should need to isn't clear – though it is able to swallow much larger animals, it eats mainly lizards and frogs. It seems unlikely that the long fangs are a defensive adaptation, because it's not a particularly irritable snake and only rarely bites in defence. Perhaps the answer is simple: it is just a big snake and so has proportionately long fangs. But then why are the king cobra's fangs so short? Unlike the gaboon viper, whose fangs collapse backwards when the snake's mouth is shut, the cobra's fangs are fixed in place. Quite simply, if they were any longer, they would puncture its lower jaw.

Greatest number of teeth

NAME **whale shark** *Rhincodon typus*

LOCATION tropical and warm temperate seas

NUMBER more than 300 rows with hundreds of teeth in each

Exactly which animal has the greatest number of teeth is a bit of a conundrum. It depends on how you define teeth, how often they are replaced and how long the animal lives. Mammals have teeth as we think of them (enamel-covered, set into the jaw and replaced only once in a lifetime), and the mammal with the biggest mouthful is probably the spinner dolphin, with up to 272. Crocodiles can have around 60 teeth, but these are replaced as many as 40 times – so that could be 2,400 teeth in a lifetime. Snails and slugs, though, have even more, if you call them teeth. They have a radula – a retractable, tongue-like file under the head – with rows of up to 27,000 microscopic teeth made of chitin, which are replaced as they wear down.

Shark teeth are specialised scales loosely embedded in a fibrous mass known as the tooth bed. In a conveyor-belt process, they are continually shed and replaced by new ones. The shark with the greatest number of teeth is probably the whale shark, which is surprising as it is mainly a giant filter feeder. It has several thousand tiny, hooked teeth, each about 2–3mm (0.08–0.12in) long, arranged in 11–12 rows on each jaw. These are probably replaced at least twice a year, and so, given that a whale shark could live as long as a human, it really does deserve the title of toothiest animal. But what it actually uses its battalion of teeth for is still a mystery.

Bamboos are strange plants. For a start, they are giant, woody grasses. Most of the 1,250 or so species do all their growing in early life. Once mature, a bamboo doesn't grow any taller, no matter how long it lives (and some survive for more than 100 years), preferring instead to send up more shoots. This means a stand of clumping bamboo, while getting no taller, can become impenetrably thick.

Flowering is eccentric, too. Many species flower only once in their lives when aged between seven and 120, and then die. And that means that every single plant of a particular species may set seed at exactly the same time and die at the same time. (This is a special problem for giant pandas, which eat virtually nothing but bamboo and face general famine every 30-80 years, when the local bamboo species flowers.)

Bamboo is also hugely important to us (there are more than 1,500 documented uses for it), and up to 40 per cent of the world's population depends on it. As for tortoiseshell bamboo, it invests a huge amount of energy in seed production but may survive flowering and is widely grown as a crop. It's one of the tallest giant bamboos and probably the fastest growing. One shoot is recorded as putting on a metre of growth in a single day – that's 4cm (1.6in) an hour – and another grew 20m (65ft 6in) in eight weeks. It really is grass that you could watch grow.

Fastest-growing plant

NAME **tortoiseshell bamboo**, or **moso**, *Phyllostachys edulis*
LOCATION China and in cultivation worldwide
ABILITY growing literally centimetres (even inches) an hour

Smallest fish

Not only is this the smallest of all fish, it's also the smallest and lightest vertebrate (animal with a backbone) yet known. It beats the previous record-holder, the Philippine Lake Buhi goby, by 0.5mm (0.02in), though females are a fraction larger. It is half the size of the two other known infantfish but with a deeper ('stouter') body. It is strange, though, not only because of its size but also because it's paedomorphic – meaning that adults resemble juveniles, hence the name infantfish. Moreover, it has no teeth, scales, pelvic fins or pigment (except in the eyes). It has large eyes, though no one knows why, as it hasn't yet been observed in the wild. Given that it has a large mouth but no teeth, it probably eats plankton.

Having fast-tracked the time needed to reach maturity by opting for a paedomorphic lifestyle and probably living for just a couple of months, this transparent, tadpole-like fish can reproduce fast and therefore might evolve fast. This could be a useful ability as it lives in protected coral lagoons comparatively free from temperature increases and storm waves – an environment that could change dramatically if global warming has its predicted effect.

Australian biologists speculate that the stout infantfish may be abundant and a significant part of a food chain, though only six individuals have been caught. That it went undiscovered in a well-studied area of the world until recently, being named only in 2004, shows just how many other marine species remain to be discovered, some of them possibly even smaller than this tiddler.

NAME **stout infantfish** *Schindleria brevipinguis*
LOCATION Great Barrier Reef, Australia
SIZE just 6.5–8.4mm (0.2–0.3in) long

All the humongous fungi records are held by underground clone colonies of species of honey fungus. The success of honey fungus lies with its 'shoestrings', or rhizomorphs – parallel hyphae (root-like extensions), covered in a tough, dark rind. These shoestrings travel huge distances in search of food – vulnerable trees or dead wood – and pass back nutrients to the main mass of hyphae, called a thallus. They penetrate the bark of a living tree, often a young one, and siphon off water and nutrients from the sapwood. If the tree doesn't defend itself properly, the rhizomorphs spread to the roots and effectively strangle the tree, extracting nutrients from the dying wood. Over the years, new colonies form, all clones of the original organism.

The largest-known mass of honey fungus, identified by DNA fingerprinting, is an *Armillaria ostoyae* clone in Oregon, 5 km (3 miles) across in some places and estimated to be at least 2,400 years old (possibly twice that age). In autumn, it sends up great masses of fruiting bodies, though the individual mushrooms are small by comparison with those of long-lived fruiting bodies of species such as the artist's fungus *Ganoderma applanatum*. Even larger honey fungus clones may exist in the huge conifer forests of Eurasia (*Armillana* particularly likes certain conifers). Though the fungus might seem monstrous, it is part of a forest recycling system, creating spaces for new plants to grow and adding organic matter to the soil that provides nutrients for the trees.

Most gargantuan of growths

NAME **honey fungus**, or **shoestring rot**, *Armillaria ostoyae*
LOCATION Malheur National Forest in the Blue Mountains, Oregon, USA
SIZE covers more than 890 hectares (2,198 acres)

The largest elephant ever recorded was a bull shot in Angola in 1974 (before the increase in poaching that decimated elephant populations). It weighed more than 12.2 tonnes (12 tons) – the equivalent of 178 men – and had a standing shoulder height of 3.96m (13ft) and a trunk-to-tail length of 10.7m (35ft). Another bull, shot in Damaraland, Namibia, in 1978, had a standing height of 4.2m (13ft 10in), but the so-called desert elephants that live there have proportionately longer legs.

The average male savannah elephant is about 3–3.7m (9ft 10in–12ft), and females are smaller. Smaller still is the forest elephant at 2–3m (6ft 7in–9ft10 in), though it's still a heavyweight at 2–4.5 tonnes (2–4.4 tons). Asian elephants are closer in weight and height to the forest elephant, though slightly taller, the highest point being the top of the head rather than the shoulder. The Asian record-holder is probably a Nepalese bull estimated to be 3.7m (12ft) at the shoulder. Only white rhinos and hippos come near such mammoths in terms of weight.

Not surprisingly, elephants hold other records, including the largest appetite of all land animals, consuming 75–150kg (165–330lb) of vegetable matter a day (double this in the case of large bulls). Despite an enormous stomach and up to about 19m (62ft) of intestines, digestion is relatively inefficient, to the benefit of the animals who feed off its faeces and the plants whose seeds it helpfully disperses in packets of fertiliser.

Heaviest land animal

NAME **African savannah elephant** *Loxodonta africana*
LOCATION Africa, south of the Sahara
SIZE 4–7 tonnes (3.9–6.9 tons)

Oldest living animal

NAME **cold-seep deep-sea tubeworm**
Lamellibrachia luymesi
LOCATION Gulf of Mexico
AGE at least 250 years

Tubeworms are best known as a group of animals that, with the aid of chemical-converting bacteria, thrive in pitch darkness around hydrothermal vents, where hot gases and fluids spew out of the sea-bottom and nourish forms of life that are found nowhere else on Earth. Some of these vents can be as hot as 400°C (750°F), and the tubeworms around them grow fast – more than a metre (3.3ft) a year (see p.64).

But not all deep-sea vents are that hot, and in fact not all of them are hot at all. There are also cold hydrocarbon seeps, for example, which release their fluid slowly and steadily and at the same cold temperature as the deep seawater. They support tubeworms, too. Some of these tubeworms can measure more than 2m (6.6ft) and appear to have taken a very long time to grow to such a length.

One year, deep in the Gulf of Mexico, scientists covered some of the tubeworms' white outer casing with blue stain and returned the next year to find less than 1cm (0.4in) of new white growth peeping through. From that – and taking into account the faster growth rate of the young tubeworms and the fact that they did not even collect the biggest and oldest animals – they calculated an individual's possible lifespan as at least 250 years. Species such as giant tortoises and bowhead whales are believed to reach ages of at least 150 and 200 years respectively. However, the only other animals that might really rival tubeworms are colonial ones such as corals, although with them it's hard to distinguish one animal from another.

Smallest reptile

NAME **Jaragua gecko** *Sphaerodactylus ariasae*

LOCATION Beata Island, Dominican Republic (Hispaniola)

SIZE just 1.4–1.8cm (0.5–0.7in) from the tip of the snout to the base of the tail

If you want to look for new species that are very small or very large, islands are where you are most likely to find them. And what better place for islands than the Caribbean? That's where the two record-holders for the world's smallest reptile have been discovered. The first is the Virgin Gorda gecko *Sphaerodactylus parthenopion*, found in 1964 on the island of Gorda in the British Virgin Islands. Then, in 1998, the Jaragua gecko was discovered on the island of Beata, part of the Dominican Republic's Jaragua National Park (after which it was named). Both the Virgin Gorda gecko and the Jaragua gecko average just 1.6cm (0.6in) from the tips of their snouts to the base of their tails.

The advantage of being small means it's easier to hide and you don't need so much to eat, making it easier to survive on an island when food is more limited. But being very, very small means having a large body surface area relative to body volume, which puts both geckos at risk of dehydration through evaporation. The Jaragua gecko survives by scurrying about in and under moist leaf litter in remnant forest on the island, eating tiny insects, spiders and mites. In fact, scientists think it has probably taken the niche that, on the mainland, would normally be filled by a spider. Though it's not technically endangered, it may soon be classified as such, because much of the forest where it lives has been logged – barely 10 per cent of the original forest remains in the West Indies.

Longest whiskers

A whisker may be just a rod of dead skin cells, but it functions as a sophisticated antenna. At its base is a blood-filled follicle, and when the whisker moves, it stimulates nerve cells. Depending on an animal's lifestyle, whiskers (vibrissae) may be any length and thickness and are usually arranged in several areas on the face: on the cheeks, on or around the nose and above the eyes.

The animals that have the longest and accomplish most with them are usually those active in darkness or in low-light conditions, which include the marine mammals. Some seal whiskers may each be serviced by more than 1,000 nerve cells (compared to about 250 for a rat). Effectively, they function as eyes and fingers. They may pick up messages not only about texture, shape and size, but also movement and water pressure, for in water any movement leaves a wake, or 'footprint', of whatever has passed by.

Antarctic fur seals do much of their hunting at night, after krill and squid, and in the Antarctic winter, night is virtually perpetual. Their whiskers are arranged in precise patterns on their cheeks, and when a fur seal is hunting, its whiskers can point forward, feeling ahead, like those of a cat when it's hunting. A bull Antarctic fur seal has the longest whiskers of all. Why, no one knows. Maybe he uses them to express his inner emotions or maybe he just needs them to look good – signalling he's a tip-top hunter when parading his prowess on the breeding grounds.

NAME	**Antarctic fur seal** *Arctocephalus gazella*
LOCATION	Antarctic waters
SIZE	35cm–50cm (13.7–19.5 in) long

Coelacanths are not only ancient but also the only surviving members of their group and among the oldest of all vertebrates (animals with backbones). They were thought to have become extinct 65 million years ago, until 1938, when a living one was hauled up in a fishing net off South Africa. Surviving populations have since been discovered throughout the western Indian Ocean (including the Comoros archipelago, Madagascar, Kenya, Tanzania, Mozambique and South Africa), and a second, related species (*Latimeria menadoensis*) was recently discovered thousands of kilometres away off Sulawesi, Indonesia.

Differing little from their ancestors, living coelacanths are up to 2m (6ft 6in) long, with seven lobed, paddle-like fins – distant relatives of the animal that took the first steps on land some 350 million years ago. No coelacanth has been observed alive at the surface, probably because the fishes live in cold, well-oxygenated water below 100m (328ft) and die at the warm surface, where there's less dissolved oxygen.

A coelacanth has the largest-known fish egg, roughly the size of a grapefruit and weighing up to 350g (12oz). The female carries as many as 26 of these at once for a gestation period of about 13 months – a heavy load indeed. It also appears to have an electrosensory organ in its snout, possibly to help it hunt in the dark, and has been observed gathering in caves and doing 'head stands'. Biologists are now using special diving techniques in an attempt to discover more about the social life of this mysterious living fossil.

Oldest surviving fish

NAME **coelacanths** *Latimeria chalumnae* and *L. menadoensis*

LOCATION western Indian Ocean and Pacific

AGE 400 million years

Largest wingspan

NAME **wandering albatross** *Diomedea exulans*

LOCATION southern oceans

SIZE up to 3.4m (11ft 1in) wide

The wanderer has the longest of all wings. They are narrow, flat, light and designed for soaring and high-speed gliding in the strong, steady winds of open oceans. It rides the waves and weather fronts and can cruise at 55kph (34mph) for hundreds of kilometres and reach 88kph (55mph) over short distances. It may not breed until it is 6–8 years old and can live to be 50 or more. It builds up a vast ocean map, learning the best foraging areas and remembering the location of its remote birth island, normally returning there every other year to display or nest – the only time it alights on land.

The smaller, lighter females can maintain maximum glide speed using lighter winds and so forage further north than the larger, heavier males, who are more energy efficient in the windier subantarctic. This allows a pair to scour a huge combined area, covering up to 13,000 km (8,060 miles) on a single trip, and cuts down on competition for food.

Large tube-nostrils enable them to locate feeding areas using scent cues – chemicals released over upwelling zones and sea mounts. An albatross's favourite food is deep-water squid, which it may catch by sitting on the sea at night, waiting for them to come up to the surface. But it's also a scavenger, often following ships for refuse and fishing scraps. And here lies its downfall. Huge numbers of wandering albatrosses drown every year scavenging bait from the hooks of longline fishing fleets, threatening the species with extinction.

Most elastic animal

NAME   **ribbonworm**, or **bootlace worm**, *Lineus longissimus*
LOCATION   northern Atlantic
SIZE   can be more than 30m (98ft 4in) long when stretched

This is not only the most elastic creature in the world, but it's also one of the most bizarre predators. It's a nemertean worm. Like many of its relatives, it is basically one long, muscular tube, with a brain but no heart. Though the more normal length of this ribbonworm is about 5-15m (16-49ft), individuals of 30m (98ft) have been recorded. The extreme-length record may, however, result from the fact that the worm can considerably elongate its body – very useful for getting under rocks and tying itself up in a knot. Like most nemertean worms, it can regenerate lost or damaged body parts should it get stretched to breaking point.

Despite its appearance, it's a hunter, searching out marine creatures such as other worms, snails, crustaceans and even fish. It can see, using a row of up to 40 small eyespots on either side of its snout, but it probably tracks prey by chemical trails rather than sight, as it is often found squirming around in dark places such as muddy gravel and under boulders. The ribbonworm's secret weapon is a powerful, long, muscular, tongue-like proboscis that it shoots out to lasso prey. The body has a purplish iridescence, making it seem even more unearthly. And it's an animal to be wary of. If you pick one up, you'll find yourself covered in thick, sticky mucus with a strange smell – a smell that could mean it's just released some of the potent tetrodotoxins it uses for defence.

Giant-snake stories abound – due to the wild imaginations of many early explorers, the difficulties in estimating or measuring the length of live animals which refuse to stay still, and the fact that large snake skins can be deliberately stretched without causing much noticeable distortion. Most modern herpetologists have a healthy scepticism about any snake claimed to be longer than 9m (30ft).

The most whopping tales concern the South American anaconda. It rarely grows longer than 6m (20ft 6in), yet is probably the subject of more exaggerated claims about size than any other animal. Anacondas spend most of their time in water and so, admittedly, can support an enormous weight (the heaviest snake ever recorded was an anaconda weighing 227kg/500lb). But the famous claim by Lt Col. Percy Fawcett in 1907 of one 18.9m (62ft) long has since been shown to be a big exaggeration.

Female reticulated pythons, though, do reach 6m (20ft) reasonably often, and as length comes with age, and constrictors tend to live a long time, exceptional lengths are feasible. In fact, the longest snake properly recorded is a female reticulated python, supposedly measuring 10m (32ft 9in), which was shot on the Indonesian island of Celebes in 1912.

A large female is sufficiently strong, long and expandable to stop the blood flow and breathing of a large mammal and swallow it whole. Indeed, there is at least one reliable record of a reticulated python with an adult human in its stomach. The top records for length, though, are still likely to remain those in the past, as most snakes, persecuted the world over, seldom get to live to a ripe old age.

Longest snake

NAME **reticulated python** *Python reticulatus*

LOCATION South-east Asia

SIZE 6m (20ft), and possibly up to 10m (32ft 9in)

Tallest living thing

NAME   **the Stratosphere Giant**, a California redwood, *Sequoia sempervirens*

LOCATION   Humboldt Redwoods State Park, California

HEIGHT   112.8m (370ft 2in)

The Stratosphere Giant may now be the tallest tree in the world – and, the tallest living organism. But the tallest ever reliably reported – the Cornthwaite Tree, a huge mountain ash in Victoria, Australia – was measured after it had been felled in 1855 as 114m (374ft). The tallest mountain ash today, growing in Tasmania, is a relatively short 97m (318ft 3in). This means that all the tallest trees now are California redwoods, and there are about two dozen taller than 110m (360ft).

Redwoods have been extensively logged, and so it's very likely that there have been taller ones than these in the past. But how much taller? According to calculations made in 2004, taking into account such factors as the pull of gravity and the limits of water friction, it's possible for a California redwood to grow to between 122m and 130m (400-426ft).

So what goes on 50 or 60 storeys up a tree? For one thing, these trees sprout whole new trees, known as reiterated trunks. One redwood studied had a whole forest in its crown – 209 reiterated trunks. Most of them were fairly small, but the largest was 2.6m (8.5ft) in diameter and 40m (131ft) tall. Deep soil had also accumulated up there, in crotches and on large branches, and growing out of it were ferns, shrubs and other trees, not necessarily redwoods. There were also plenty of insects and earthworms, molluscs and even a sizeable population of salamanders.

Identifying the biggest brain of all is a bit of a brainteaser, depending on whether you mean just largest or biggest as in brainiest. And is brain size actually linked to intelligence? You really need to be a brain scientist to be exact about the matter.

Big animals, of course, have big brains. The sperm whale brain weighs in at a massive 7.8kg (17.2lb), while the biggest land animal, the African elephant (see p.170), has the biggest terrestrial brain – up to 5.4kg (11.9lb). By comparison, a human brain is relatively small. But relative to body size, it's actually bigger. So does that mean that humans are top of the intelligence league? This is where it gets complicated. If we take intelligence to mean the ability to reason, and the degree of complexity of the neocortex (an area of a mammal brain involved in thought and communication) being an indication of that ability, then humans win outright. But the role of the neocortex is still being investigated, and as far as many experts are concerned, our brain should still be regarded as merely a big version of a primate one.

Some scientists, though, believe our brain has undergone more rapid evolution than that of any other animal, fuelled by the development of highly complex social structures and behaviour. For instance, we've developed the ability to deceive others – and even ourselves. And despite what evidence about the state of the world might suggest, the human brain may, according to one theory, still be evolving at speed. Makes you think.

Biggest brain

NAME **human** *Homo sapiens*

SIZE 1.3kg (2.9lb) on average

ABILITY thinking

Ants are arguably the most successful animals on Earth, estimated to comprise 15 per cent of the planet's total biomass. It's all due to cooperation: individuals take roles and work as if cells in one superorganism. Members of a colony are offspring of the queen, and in evolutionary terms, it makes sense to sacrifice individuality in order to help their relatives. Some ants, however, are taking such togetherness to the extreme.

In the 1900s, a tiny, brown, innocuous ant stowed away among plant material being exported on boats from South America to the US and as far afield as South Africa and Australia. These original Argentine colonisers were few in number, but their tiny genetic stock has led to big things. In new, warm lands, without their South American parasites and with no significant check on numbers other than availability of water, they have multiplied, outcompeting native ants by sheer mass. The largest supercolony of all is composed of millions of genetically related and interconnected nests and stretches at least 6,000km (3,720 miles) from northern Italy to northern Spain.

The ants' success lies in fecundity (nests have numerous queens and so breed fast) and peace. Unlike nests of native populations, they don't bother fighting each other, which leaves more time for food gathering, reproduction and defence. This unusual social organisation is unlikely to be watered down by new Argentine ant arrivals, as any ants not recognised as close relatives are attacked. And so the supercolonies, from California to Australia, are likely to grow and grow, with new ones forecast for Asia.

Largest superorganism

NAME **Argentine ant** *Linepithema humile*
LOCATION has spread to six continents
ABILITY forming supercolonies of billions of ants

Longest tongue

NAME   **Morgan's Madagascan sphinx moth** *Xanthopan morganii praedicta*

LOCATION   Madagascar

SIZE   a proboscis 30–35cm (12–14in) long – the longest-known 'tongue' relative to body size

This is probably the most famous of tongue of all. It was first brought to the attention of the scientific world through the imagination of Charles Darwin, the great 19th-century natural philosopher and father of evolution. In 1862, he examined a specimen of the comet orchid which grows in the forest canopy in Madagascar. It has large, waxy, white, star-shaped flowers that produce a powerful, sweet scent at night. What fascinated Darwin was that its nectar was at the bottom of a spur around 30cm (12in) long and he was convinced that the structures and pollination devices of orchids had developed in tandem with their insect pollinators.

Knowing that white, night-scented flowers attracted moths, he wrote in 1877: 'In Madagascar there must be moths with proboscides [the 'tongues' through which they drink nectar] capable of extension to a length of between ten and eleven inches!' As the flower offered insects no landing pad, it was likely to be a hovering hawkmoth. Darwin was ridiculed for his suggestion. But in 1903, Morgan's Madagascan sphinx moth was discovered, with a proboscis to match the length of the spur.

For many years, the relationship between the two species in the wild was unconfirmed, but the moth has recently been observed visiting the orchid flowers and carrying away pollen. There remains a further mystery, though. The comet orchid's close relative, *Angraecum longicalcar*, has a spur measuring 40cm (16in), indicating that there is another moth yet to be discovered with an even longer tongue.

Most numerous animal

These are the most numerous multicellular animals and are outnumbered only by single-celled bacteria. What they demonstrate is that, to be a multicellular animal, you don't really need a whole lot: an outer surface, muscle, a nerve or two, a mouth, a gut, a way of excreting and a way of reproducing. That's about all most nematodes have, and with those basics, they're as compact as an animal can be and have become the most successful on Earth – in fact, probably four out of five of all animals.

If you pick up a handful of soil, you'd also be holding thousands of worm-shaped nematodes. In an acre of rich farmland, there can be 3 billion. There are nematodes at the poles and at the deepest point on the seabed. If conditions ever get too hot or cold or dry, they can suspend animation, shutting down all body functions until things get better. There are also more different species of nematode than in any other phylum except the arthropods (insects, spiders and their relatives): 20,000 nematode species have been described, but that's hardly a start. Most of the ones scientists know best are microscopic parasites, on humans or on other animals or plants, but there's probably not a creature on the planet that isn't parasitised by one. It's as parasites, especially intestinal ones, that nematodes become large, and the larger the host, the larger they will grow. One found in a sperm whale measured 8m (26ft) in length.

NAME **nematodes** in the phylum Nemata
LOCATION everywhere – in the sea, on land and in you
NUMBER billions of billions – probably four out of five animals

This is a multiple record-beater among birds. It's not only the tallest and the heaviest but also the fastest runner with the largest eyes and the biggest egg. Being a herbivore (plant eater) and very large means that it needs to spend most of its time eating, and it travels many kilometres a day to get its fill. When it flees from predators, its huge thighs are capable of powering it at up to 72kph (45mph), aided by antelope-like, two-toed feet (other birds have four toes).

Its scientific name, *camelus,* probably refers to the fact that it can get by with little water, making use of moisture in succulents and other plants and, aided by its long windpipe, saving water by cooling inhaled air so it contains less moisture when exhaled. Huge wings also act as sunshades and fans, and a comparatively featherless neck and legs can lose heat fast.

Though it can defend itself with its powerful legs, it's a gentle creature – unlike Stirton's thunderbird, the largest bird that ever lived. This flightless Australian giant was more than 3m tall (nearly 10ft) and weighed 500kg (1,105lb). Nicknamed the 'giant demon duck of doom' on account of its duck-ish ancestory and huge bill, this was almost certainly a bird with a taste for bone-cracking. Bird-headed, kangaroo-like giant creatures feature in prehistoric Aboriginal paintings and might just be pictures of this nightmare creature, though it probably became extinct some 26,000 years ago.

Biggest bird

NAME	**ostrich** *Struthio camelus*
LOCATION	drier regions of Africa south of the Sahara
SIZE	up to 2.8m (9ft) tall and 160kg (353lb) in weight

The blue whale has the largest clutch of superlatives in the animal world, including the heaviest body, the loudest voice, the biggest appetite and the smallest prey (in relation to body size). It's also one of the most mysterious animals – despite its phenomenal size, we know surprisingly little about many aspects of its life. It grows to an average of 24–27m (78.7–88.5ft) long, with a maximum-recorded, world-record length of more than 33m (110ft) and a record-breaking weight of 190 tonnes (187 tons).

It seems surprising that it can be so big when it eats tiny, shrimp-like creatures called krill, but a blue whale gulps down about four tonnes or more of these highly nutritious crustaceans a day. With the loudest voice in the animal kingdom, its low-frequency sounds can travel literally hundreds or even thousands of kilometres, though no one knows whether such powerful vocalisations are used to communicate over great distances or for underwater imaging to help with long-distance navigation.

The blue's size and speed saved it in the days of sail-boat whaling, but one of the grimmest blue whale facts is that more than 350,000 were killed following mechanisation of the whaling fleets during the 20th century. Almost all populations were drastically reduced in size, some by 99 per cent. Now the hunting of blue whales is banned, but only the population that summers off California seems to be thriving. Elsewhere in the world, there is serious concern about the future of these remarkable giants.

Largest animal ever

NAME	**blue whale** *Balaenoptera musculus*
LOCATION	ocean-wide
SIZE	the largest animal ever to have lived

These jellyfish relatives are so primitive – one first appeared 650 million years ago – that they are not even considered single animals but, rather, colonies of five types of organism: float, sensory, stinging, digestive and reproductive. The tentacles come in two sizes – short ones massed under the float and one or several (depending on the species) extremely long, trailing ones for deeper fishing. Sometimes these tentacles will stretch outwards on the surface and sometimes in opposite directions, and when they do they make the man-o'-war, at least temporarily, longer than a blue whale and thus the longest animal on the planet (putting aside the 'elastic' ribbonworm – see p.182).

Most of the time, though, these long tentacles hang down. When touched or stimulated by chemicals such as animal proteins, their tiny stinging cells (nematocysts) release barbed threads that puncture skin and inject nerve poison. A small fish that bumps into a tentacle is immediately paralysed and held, while muscles at the top contract to haul up the catch. Then the fish is engulfed and bathed in enzymes, which break it down into nutrients for distribution to the other members of the colony.

The notoriety of the Portuguese man-o'-war, as far as humans are concerned, lies in its randomness. It hunts randomly and goes wherever the winds and ocean currents take it. That can often be inshore waters or a beach. When it's beached, of course, it dies, but the nematocysts keep on working, inflicting excruciating stings on thousands of people every year.

Longest weapons

NAME	**Portuguese man-o'-war**, or **bluebottle**, *Physalia* species
LOCATION	tropical and sub-tropical open oceans
LENGTH	stinging tentacles up to 35m (116ft) long

Oldest living clone

NAME **King's holly** *Lomatia tasmanica*

LOCATION just one gully in south-west Tasmania

AGE more than 43,600 years old

This remarkable shrub was discovered around 70 years ago by self-taught naturalist Deny King, while panning for tin on a mountain range in south-west Tasmania. But that area was later burnt, and the plant was never seen again. Then, in 1965, King found another population in a cool, rainforest site on a range further east. It was confirmed as a new species, a member of the Proteaceae family (with its closest relative in Chile, hinting at the time when Australia and South America were joined together), and was named in King's honour.

The plant is sterile, being genetically triploid (having three pairs of chromosomes instead of two). Since it cannot reproduce sexually, its attractive red flowers never set seed, and it can regenerate only by shooting from root suckers. This also means that all 600 or so plants in the population are genetically identical clones.

Even more extraordinary, fossil leaves of the species collected in the same region and visually identical to living leaves have been radiocarbon-dated as at least 43,600 years old. Because of this and because it reproduces clonally, biologists believe the living King's holly plant and the fossil to be, for all practical purposes, the same plant. This makes the species the oldest-known clone, beating the creosote bush (at 11,700 years) and the previous record-holder, the North American huckleberry (at about 12,000 years). It was alive when *Homo sapiens* and Neanderthal man existed together, but tragically, this ancient survivor is now threatened with extinction.

Longest hair

NAME **muskox** *Ovibos moschatus*

LOCATION Arctic Alaska, Canada, Greenland, Europe

LENGTH up to 90cm (2ft 9in) long

That famous naked ape, *Homo sapiens*, can grow hair longer than 5m (16ft 5in), the world record being 5.15m (16ft 11in). But human hair is more for sexual display than warmth, the usual function of hair. So maybe the record should really be for the longest known body-warming hair. And the muskox coat is certainly warm – many times warmer than the coats of any of its relatives, sheep and goats.

Muskoxen, in fact, have two coats – the long shaggy one that hangs down almost to the ground and a fine, short, very warm undercoat, as much as 30cm (12in) thick in places, called (in Inuit) the qiviut. The two coats together get muskoxen through winters as cold as –70°C (–94°F). Such super-insulation also allows them to lower their metabolism by about 20 per cent, to help them get by on much less food during the long, dark, freezing-cold winters.

If the muskox looks like a tundra mammal from the last ice age – something that might have gone the way of the woolly mammoth – that's because it is. It shared the tundra with the mammoth and, along with a few other mammals, survived the new, warm era by adapting to climate changes, sticking close to the rim of the Arctic Ocean and not migrating. Much later, the arrival of men with guns almost finished it off, but it was rescued by eleventh-hour conservation efforts and has now been reintroduced back into some of its old haunts.

Hairiest animal

NAME **sea otter** *Enhydra lutris*

LOCATION coastal Pacific waters

NUMBER up to 394,000 hairs a square centimetre (almost a million per square inch)

A sea otter spends most of its time on its back, at sea, resting, grooming or feeding – cracking open shellfish on an anvil it places on its tummy. It therefore needs to be both buoyant and ultra-warm. To maintain its body temperature, it burns calories at nearly three times the rate we do and so every day has to eat at least a quarter of its body weight in fish and shellfish. Blubber, used by most sea mammals for insulation, would make a sea otter too heavy to float. Instead it invests in the thickest coat of any animal, comprising up to a billion hairs.

A fine, downy undercoat traps air for insulation and is overlain by long guard hairs measuring 3.5cm (1.4in) and providing a covering so dense that water doesn't penetrate it. To keep the coat in perfect condition, the otter spends up to half of the day grooming: combing out dirt, straightening and aligning the hairs, blowing air into the undercoat and spreading waterproof oil.

A baby sea otter is born in a flotation jacket – a buoyant undercoat – and can't dive for a couple of months until this has been replaced by adult fur. However, the sea otter's luxurious coat has nearly been its downfall. Fur-hunters brought the species close to extinction, and though it is protected today, oil spills pose a new hazard. Once an otter's coat is contaminated by this oil, it loses its insulation, and the otter dies of hypothermia or from oil ingested as it tries to clean itself.

Biggest mouth

The biggest mouths are found in the sea. The widest belongs to the whale shark (see p.162), and the biggest food scoop of all is the huge, pleated throat of the blue whale (see p.198). Both animals are effectively filter-feeders, eating relatively tiny prey. The most dramatic large mouths, though, are those which engulf large animals whole and probably belong to deep-sea creatures such as the gulper or the loosejaw – elongated animals with huge (relative to size), hinged jaws.

But when it comes to mouth relative to body size, they cannot compare to the beroid comb jellies (ctenophores). A beroe is, effectively, an enormous stomach surrounded by a thin, muscular, gelatinous wall, which opens wide by means of a huge mouth. It swims by beating eight rows of ciliary comb plates along its sides, has light sensors but no eyes and can probably 'smell' its prey.

While it's cruising, a beroe's lips are held tightly shut with adhesive strips. As soon as a beroe bumps into prey, anything from other comb jellies to fish, its giant nerve net instantly triggers the lips to part, and muscles snap open the mouth at incredible speed, enabling it to engulf the creature whole. If the prey is too large to swallow, the beroe bites off a huge chunk with the thousands of sharp-tipped tiny 'teeth' (macrocilia), that line its lips and may extend into its stomach. The lips then reseal the mouth-of-all-mouths, and the bloated beroe swims away to digest its enormous meal.

NAME **beroid comb jellies** *Beroe* species

LOCATION most oceans

SIZE 5–30cm (2–11.7in) long (or wide) – all stomach and mouth

Most feathers

NAME	**tundra swan** *Cygnus columbianus*
LOCATION	North America
NUMBER	25,216 feathers

Back in 1933, a group of birdwatchers decided to count the feathers on a dead tundra swan. The amazing thing – apart from the fact that they really did spend hours counting – is that they found 20,177 of them on the swan's head and neck alone. In fact, many birds may have more than a third of their feathers here (principally 'underdown'), perhaps to protect their brains against temperature extremes when they fly very high.

Tundra swans pair for life and so don't need to grow display plumage every year to attract new sexual partners. But they do feed on water and so preen constantly, using oil from a gland at the base of the tail to keep their plumage flexible, insulated and waterproof. They also need to replace worn feathers. The adults moult their 'primaries', or flight feathers, simultaneously from July to mid-August, while on their Arctic breeding grounds and before they start their long south-bound migration in autumn. But the remainder of their thousands of feathers are lost gradually, from summer to the following spring. So, though you might find quill feathers at a nest, or a lakeside moulting ground where non-breeding-birds gather, you will never find more than a tiny proportion of a tundra swan's 25,000 body feathers at any one site.

The bird that holds the record for the least number of feathers is supposedly a ruby-throated hummingbird, with 940. But relative to body size, this tiny species has a lot more feathers than a tundra swan, which is about 2,000 times larger in size.

Evolution often has a way of giving certain animals a monopoly on one aspect of their environment, and giraffes are a very visible example of that. No other large mammal, bar the occasional elephant, can browse the higher reaches of the acacia trees that provide the basis of a giraffe's diet. Its sensitive and dextrous lips and long (45cm/18in), prehensile tongue are also designed for the task of carefully stripping out leaves from their thorny protection. In this way, a giraffe can get about 34kg (75lb) of virtually uncontested, nutritious leaves a day. It also obtains enough moisture from its diet to survive without drinking. If there is an opportunity to drink, it has to spread its front legs wide, get its head down and rely on a complicated series of vascular valves to keep its blood from rushing down there, too.

Its height, size and excellent vision mean that an adult giraffe is not an easy animal to ambush in the day, and other animals may even use giraffes as predator look-outs. Lions, however, are a threat, especially at night. Because, after dark, a giraffe's height and vision are of limited use and it's lying down and ruminating (chewing unprocessed food stored in a special part of its stomach). Giraffes are, though, capable of giving a powerful kick. And should one sense lions in time, it can gallop away, with a rolling, leggy gait that belies its speed: 50–60kph (31–37mph).

Tallest animal

NAME	**giraffe** *Giraffa camelopardalis*
LOCATION	Africa south of the Sahara
SIZE	males up to 5.5m (18ft) high

Nature is full of weapons – horns, antlers and tusks among them – grown by males for fighting over or merely impressing females. But only one animal develops such a weapon from a single, long tooth. This is the narwhal. The male's tusk, which pierces its upper lip, is actually its upper left front tooth. Instead of staying embedded in the gum, as it does in females, it pushes out through the upper lip, twisting (always counter-clockwise when viewed from the root) as it grows, into a lance with an average length of 2m (6ft 7in) – roughly half the length of the whale's body. Exceptional tusks can be as long as 3m (9ft 10in) and weigh up to 10kg (22lb). They look rather like gnarled, twisted walking sticks.

The role of the tusk baffled scientists for years. Among many theories were that it was used for spearfishing, grubbing for food and drilling through ice. In fact, males have been observed crossing tusks at the surface, and the presence of scars and wounds around the head region, combined with the high incidence of broken tusks, suggests that they are used for fighting and as displays of strength. The narwhal's tusk was thought to have been the horn of the legendary unicorn until early in the 17th century, and traders and chemists conspired to keep the existence of the whale a secret while selling 'unicorn horns' with magical healing properties for immense profit. Queen Elizabeth I paid £10,000 for one.

Most impressive tooth

NAME	**narwhal** *Monodon monoceros*
LOCATION	Arctic waters
LENGTH	a spiralling front tooth up to 3m (9ft 10in) long

These eyes belong to a formidable predator that hunts in the dark depths of the coldest of oceans. Since few adult specimens have so far been examined, exactly how it uses its huge, protruding eyes is not known. But it can light up its surroundings by literally glowing, enabling it to focus its dinner-plate-sized eyes on fast-moving prey such as the large Patagonian toothfish – which the only intact specimen, an immature female, was snacking on when it was caught in 2003 by fishermen in the Ross Sea.

Large eyes go with the most massive body of any known invertebrate – even larger than the better-known giant squid. The Ross Sea specimen weighed 150kg (331lb 5oz) and was, with its tentacles stretched out, nearly 5.4m (17ft 7in), with a massive 2.5m (8ft 2in) mantle (body) and huge head. In fact, the species may grow up to 15m (49ft), with a mantle up to 4m (13ft). Unlike giant squid, it has a physiology that suggests it can move fast, a large muscular fin and up to 25 razor-sharp and swivelling hooks on clubs at the ends of its two extended tentacles. It also has a huge, parrot-like beak, making it one of the most fearsome predators in the sea.

Largest eyes

NAME **colossal squid** *Mesonychoteuthis hamiltoni* (the photo shows a model)

LOCATION deep, cold oceans

SIZE 60cm (24in) or wider

This is one huge tree complex – a giant stand of genetically identical tree trunks connected by a common root system and weighing thousands of tonnes – called Pando, or 'I spread', in Latin. Though the individual trees, or ramets, are comparatively short lived, there are at least 47,000 of them, all males, and the clone itself is at least 10,000 years old. It may even be a lot, lot older. And though the ramets are comparatively slender and seldom get to be very tall, the area the tree complex covers is at least 43 hectares (106 acres).

The quaking aspen can reproduce in a normal, sexual way, producing seeds. But if conditions are not good for seed germination or if the aspen is damaged by fire or an avalanche, it opts for fast, vegetative reproduction, throwing out new suckers to replace fallen trees and continue the spread of the organism. In fact, being partially fire-proof, it thrives on periodic fires, which kill off competing trees.

A mature root system like that of the giant clone is also capable of putting out nearly half a million shoots a hectare (nearly a quarter of a million an acre), and since aspen shoots can grow a metre a season, it can out-compete other trees. As a result, the quaking aspen successfully colonised North America in the wake of the last ice age and is now the most widely distributed tree on the continent and the second only to juniper as the most widespread tree in the world.

Heaviest living thing

NAME	**quaking aspen**, or **American aspen** *Populus tremuloides*
LOCATION	Wasatch Mountains, Utah, USA
SIZE	6,000 tonnes (5,900 tons)

Fattest carnivore

NAME **polar bear** *Ursus maritimus*
LOCATION Arctic and subarctic
ABILITY a female is capable of putting on four times her weight in a season

Polar bears are large. Their average weight is an impressive 200–600kg (442–1,326lb), but there is an unsubstantiated record of a male allegedly shot in Alaska that weighed a whopping 1,002kg (2,210lb). By comparison, the most heavily-built bears – grizzlies from the Gulf of Alaska called Kodiak bears – have a record weight of only 751kg (1,656lb).

Pregnant female polar bears spend most of the autumn and early winter asleep and most of their waking time searching for food (mainly fat-rich seals and their pups). By the end of a good spring, they can sometimes have fat deposits amounting to more than 50 per cent of their body weight. This makes them the record-holders for the greatest fat intake of any adult land mammal. Females are smaller than males, yet their seasonal increase in weight is no less than four times greater. During winter sleep, a female polar bear has a lower metabolic rate and reduced heart and breathing rates, and she doesn't eat, drink, urinate or defecate. But her body is fuelled by fat reserves and her temperature rarely drops more than a few degrees below normal.

Unfortunately, climate change is causing the pack ice on which polar bears hunt to freeze later and thaw earlier. This makes hunting difficult and, consequently, the average weight of polar bears in some populations is decreasing. Scientists are worried that, in the future, females may not be able to put on enough weight to survive both their winter sleep and the effort of rearing of young cubs.

There are three known species of thresher shark – the common, the bigeye and the pelagic – and there is also some evidence of a fourth from Baja California, in Mexico, which is yet to be described and named. But the common thresher is the largest and has the longest tail, or caudal, fin – possibly up to 3m (10ft) long in the biggest individuals.

All threshers have the same basic shape, though, and the exceptionally long upper lobe of the scythe-like tail is almost a tail in itself. It's not the longest fin in the world – that probably belongs to the humpback whale (see p32), which has enormous pectoral fins, or flippers, that can be more than 5m (16ft 6in) long. But it's the longest relative to body size.

The thresher is believed to use its fin as a whip, by swimming around a shoal of small fish or squid in ever-decreasing circles and then using it to stun or kill the frightened animals with a hefty whack. Threshers have been seen killing seabirds in this way, but few of these sharks have been observed feeding under water, and so there is actually little direct evidence to support this intriguing theory. In some parts of the world, however, killer whales (see p.48) use a similar technique, and anglers have reported catching thresher sharks on live baits – not hooked in the mouth, but in the tail. Like sharks the world over, threshers are fished for the commercial value of their fins, used to make expensive shark-fin soup.

Longest fin

NAME **common thresher shark** *Alopias vulpinus*

LOCATION tropical and temperate oceans

SIZE up to 6m (20ft) long, almost half of which is tail fin

Largest flower

NAME   **Rafflesia** *Rafflesia arnoldii*

LOCATION   Borneo and Sumatra

SIZE   up to 0.9m (3ft) in diameter, 11kg (25lb)

The flower is all you'll ever see of a Rafflesia, because the rest of this intriguing plant is comprised of just threads inside a tropical vine. It is a slow-growing parasite, totally dependent on *Tetastigma* vines, from which it draws nutrients.

It is very rare for a rafflesia bud to emerge from its host on the forest floor, and about nine months pass before it swells to the point when it literally bursts open. Its five fleshy lobes (red sepals) curl back to release a putrid stench like rotting meat and reveal the huge, open-topped dome that houses the reproductive parts (which can be either female or male). The smell attracts carrion-loving beetles and flies. As the pollinators don't fly far, flowers need to be nearby and flowering synchronised so pollen can be moved from male to female flowers within just a few days. How this happens is a mystery. Another mystery is how any of its thousands of tiny seeds land on a vine, though it's possible they get there via the dung of the tree shrews and squirrels that eat the fruit. Somehow, a seed penetrates the stem and starts growing. But it will be years before it buds.

Rafflesia's scientific name commemorates two famous 19th-century plant and animal collectors – Sir Stanford Raffles, founder of Singapore, and botanist Joseph Arnold. Sadly, as its host is disappearing with its shrinking rainforest home, Rafflesia itself is fast becoming history.

Smallest amphibian

NAME   **Mount Iberia frog** *Eleutherodactylus iberia*

LOCATION   Cuba

SIZE   just 1cm (0.4in) long

If you are Brazilian, you'll claim the Brazilian gold frog as the smallest. If you're Cuban, you'll claim the Mount Iberia frog. Both average about 1 cm (0.4in) long. But given that Cuba has several other close contenders for the title – including the Tetas de Julia frog, named after the mountains on which it was found (literally 'breasts of Julia' frog), and the more aptly-named yellow-striped pygmy frog – it seems fair to give the record to Cuba. It is certainly the place of tiny frogs. In fact, Cuba has a third of the Caribbean's amphibians and an astonishing 94 per cent of these are found nowhere else in the world – though many are threatened by deforestation, exotic invaders such as rats and cats, or mining.

The Mount Iberia frog was discovered in 1993 by Cuban biologist Alberto Estrada on an expedition in search of the exceedingly rare ivory-billed woodpecker (he was probably the last person to glimpse the huge bird in Cuba, in 1986, though it has since been rediscovered in Arkansas, in the United States). He located the frog by its 'hissing' call (in the process of miniaturisation, its 'larynx' has become tiny and it has lost a few teeth). When he saw its metallic copper stripes and purple belly, he felt sure it was a species new to science. Most biologists now consider it to be the world's tiniest tetrapod – meaning it's the tiniest of all four-legged animals with a backbone.

Washed-up specimens of this serpent-like fish are reputed to be the origin of at least some sea-monster sightings. Though this shimmering, ribbon-like creature has been seen swimming close to the surface, it most probably lives in deeper water, and so most of its behaviour and life history remains a mystery. It has no tail, but running the entire length of its body is a dorsal fin (described as bright red in near-surface and beached specimens) that undulates. The oarfish appears to use this fin for hovering, and it has been seen to swim vertically up and down in the water – highly unusual for a fish. Two long pelvic fins, each reduced to a single ray and ending in a yellow and blue tassel, are held out like oars.

The few people who have seen an oarfish swimming say it moves fast, and one person even describes it as curious. It has large eyes, reminiscent of deep-sea predators. Being toothless, it's perfectly harmless to humans, and some people believe it's a filter-feeder. It does, though, have a comparatively large, protrudable mouth and is presumably capable of sucking in small shrimps, fish and squid. It may be that the tassels on its rays and the long, antennae-like spines on its head are fishing lures or sensitive feelers, and so it may hang in wait for prey, its fine-scaled, silver body reflecting the blue of the sea and making it nearly invisible. The oarfish must certainly be a puzzle to predators used to horizontal fish, especially if it decides to escape, vertically, tail first, at speed – an awesome sight indeed.

Most elongated fish

NAME	**oarfish** *Regalecus glesne*
LOCATION	worldwide in temperate and tropical seas
SIZE	up to 15.2m (50ft) long

Baggiest animal

NAME	**giant Titicaca frog** *Telmatobius culeus*
LOCATION	Lake Titicaca, Andes (Peru/Bolivia)
ABILITY	breathing through its baggy skin

Large lakes cut off from other bodies of water are like isolated oceanic islands, where species can evolve independently of evolution happening anywhere else on the planet. One of the world's most isolated lakes is Titicaca, in the Andes, which is fed just by snowmelt and rain – not by sizeable rivers.

At an altitude of 3,815 m (12,516 ft), the 8,340 sq km (3,220 sq miles) lake is also one of the world's highest and as such has a very low oxygen content. So the most important adaptation of the lake's aquatic animals (and they are almost all exclusive to Titicaca) is an exceptional ability to process what little oxygen there is. Among these is the giant Titicaca frog, one of the few amphibians that never needs to surface for air. Though it does have rudimentary lungs and can breathe air if it has to, for the most part it stays underwater, absorbing oxygen through its skin. And the more skin it has, the more oxygen it can absorb.

So, entirely as an aid to respiration, its skin hangs off it in great flabby folds and adds up to more than twice as much as the frog would need if its skin were skin-tight. It is, incidentally, among the world's largest frogs, with one having been recorded at 50cm (20in) and 1kg (2.2lb). The larger the frog becomes the proportionately more skin it needs to get enough oxygen. This means that the biggest Titicaca frogs are also the baggiest.

This plant is essentially just a pair of leaves on a short, bowl-like stem. Individuals get to be very, very old. Their strap-like leaves grow and grow and don't drop off. But they do get thrashed by the wind and so are never longer than about 6m (20ft) – rather than the 200m (656ft) they could grow to be – and are sometimes terribly split and tangled.

Welwitschia usually grows near enough to the coast to make use of the fog that rolls in from the Atlantic Ocean at night. Moisture condenses on the leaves and is both channelled down to the root and taken in through the breathing pores, or stomates. Sometimes welwitschia conserves water with a special method of photosynthesis (the way plants make food). The leaves open their stomates and take in carbon dioxide, not in the day, as do most other plants, but at night, when temperatures are coolest and they won't lose water through transpiration (evaporation through the stomates). They then store the carbon atoms as special acids until the sun's up and they can photosynthesise – using the light to synthesise the carbon into carbohydrates.

Instead of flowers, welwitschia produces cones like other gymnosperms (conifers, ginkgoes, cycads and seed ferns). These are either male ones with pollen or female ones that form the seeds. Both produce a sticky fluid – in the case of females, to capture pollen, and in the case of males, to attract insects to disperse pollen – a combination of characteristics of both flowering and non-flowering plants.

Oldest leaves

NAME **welwitschia**, or **tweeblarkanniedood** (two-leaf-cannot-die), *Welwitschia mirabilis*
LOCATION Namib Desert, south-west Africa
AGE can live to be more than 1,500 years old

Rarest animal

This is the only remaining Pinta Island Galapagos giant tortoise, and you can't get much rarer than that. It was always island wildlife that suffered the most, because isolated islands with unique species were seen by ships' crews as convenient mid-ocean supply stops. To 19th-century sailors, the huge tortoises on Pinta and other Galapagos islands were very handy: each animal was worth many meals, and one could live for up to a year without being fed. Then goats were released on Pinta as a future food source, and they stripped the island of the tortoises' staple plants.

The last Pinta tortoise was seen in 1906 – until George was found in 1971. He's about 80 now, residing at the Darwin Research Center on Santa Cruz Island. But George is a subspecies, and there are still giant tortoises on other islands. So what is the rarest whole species?

It could be the Yangtze river dolphin, which is so rare only a handful of individuals (if any) survive. The last known Hawaiian po'ouli, a small brown and black bird, died in 2004, but it's not certain if others survive or not. And there was the 1984 case of the world's most surprised ornithologist: he was smacked in the head one night by a Fiji petrel, a bird last seen in 1855. Other petrels have been spotted since, but no one knows exactly how few remain. Sadly, the list of possibilities is almost endless.

NAME	**Lonesome George** *Geochelone nigra abingdoni*
LOCATION	originally from Pinta Island, Galapagos; now on Santa Cruz
STATUS	just one individual left

There is considerable debate over which species is the record-holder, but the mammal with the smallest head-to-body length is a bumblebee-sized South-east Asian bat, which is also one of the rarest bats in the world. It was only discovered in 1973, by Dr Kitti Thonglongya (hence its alternative common name, which also refers to its pig-like nose) in limestone caves in Thailand, and another population has since been discovered in Burma.

Because so few individuals have been weighed and measured, it's difficult to be exact about dimensions. But it would seem to be slightly heavier than the other contender for 'smallest mammal', the widespread Savi's pigmy shrew, which weighs just 1.2–2.7g (0.4–0.9oz) and is 3.6–5.3cm (1.4–2.1in) long, not counting the tail (the bumblebee bat has no tail as such).

Being so small is a problem for both mammals, as they have large body-surface areas relative to body volume, resulting in great heat (energy) loss. They therefore need to eat a lot frequently. Both are voracious hunters, the bat catching mainly flies and the shrew chasing anything small enough or slow enough to tackle. To aid their frantic lifestyles, they have huge and very fast-beating hearts and special fast-contracting muscles. But if it gets cold or food is scarce, both opt for the same survival option – they become torpid and wait until conditions improve.

Tiniest mammal

NAME **bumblebee bat**, or **Kitti's hog-nosed bat**,
Craseonycteris thonglongyai

LOCATION Thailand and Burma

SIZE just 2.9–3.3cm (1.14–1.30in) long,
weighing just 1.7–3g (0.06–0.11oz)

Oldest surviving seed plant

NAME   **ginkgo**, or **maidenhair tree**, *Ginkgo biloba*

LOCATION   originally throughout northern temperate zone; now in gardens and streets

AGE   the genus dates back 280 million years

This tree is the ultimate survivor. When Hiroshima was bombed in August 1945, virtually every plant in the city was destroyed, including a particular ginkgo tree, which was burnt and irradiated. In the spring of 1946, the remains of that tree produced one sprout. Today it's a perfectly healthy tree growing in the grounds of a temple 1km (0.6 miles) from the centre of the blast.

Ginkgoes pre-date lots of things – flowers, for instance. When ginkgoes first appeared on Earth, 280 million years ago, there were no angiosperms – no plants that produced flowers and encased their seeds in fruit. In fact, as a member of the Ginkgoaceae family – the last survivor – *Ginkgo biloba* is somewhere between the primeval cycads, conifers and primitive ferns and the first flowering plants. This species has held on through Earth-shaking volcanic cataclysms, asteroid collisions and the general environmental change that caused all the plants that were the ginkgo's early contemporaries to die out or evolve into something else.

Its real problems were ice ages. It was frozen out of North America 7 million years ago and Europe 3 million years ago. But ice never reached parts of south-eastern China, and that was where they enlisted the help of a very newly evolved species – *Homo sapiens*. Trees were found by the ancient Chinese and cultivated in their temple gardens. Now, though probably extinct in the wild, they thrive in cities all over the world because of their resistance to air pollution and disease.

This is the world's biggest reptile, weighing up to 1,200kg (2,646lb). Male saltwater crocodiles are mature at about 3.2m (10ft 6in), and the smaller females at 2.2m (7ft 3in), but they continue to grow and may live to be a hundred years old. The longest authenticated record is of a male at just over 7m (23ft). But a fairly reliable record does exist from the 1950s of a beast of over 10 m (33ft) that lived along the Segama River in Sabah, Borneo – its length measured from its impression in the sand. These days, though, huge individuals longer than 6m (20ft) are rare.

A saltwater crocodile's eyes, ears and nostrils are positioned on top of its enormous head, allowing it to lie in wait for prey with the bulk of its body hidden below the surface of the water. Massive jaw muscles enable it to exert a tonne of force - enough to crush and lock its interlocking teeth on to prey – and since it can remain under water for hours, it can easily drown large mammals.

Being an indiscriminate feeder, taking anything from fish and birds to other crocodiles and mammals, a saltwater crocodile will eat people. A male protecting his territory or a female guarding her young may also be aggressive if disturbed. And so in areas where people live and bathe in waters where there are crocodiles, attacks on humans are common. It's the reptile to treat with the greatest respect.

Largest reptile

NAME	**saltwater** or **estuarine crocodile** *Crocodylus porosus*
LOCATION	fresh water, but also brackish and salt water; from India to South-east Asia and Australasia
SIZE	up to a maximum 10m (33ft) long

Heaviest tree dweller

NAME	**orang-utan** *Pongo pygmaeus*
LOCATION	Sumatra and Borneo
SIZE	males can be up to 135kg (300lb)

Life in the trees is something that's normally reserved for lighter mammals – partly because the heavier you are, the fewer branches there are that can support you, and partly because heavier mammals tend not to have the nimbleness that tree-top navigation usually requires. But primates evolved in the trees. Climbing, after all, is what hands are for, and recognising fruit is the original reason for primates developing colour vision.

The larger great apes have, though, in part, left the branches for the ground. Lesser apes, the gibbons, are superb tree-climbers, but apes that are bigger – chimpanzees, bonobos (see p.299) and gorillas – have lost much of the knack. Pygmy chimps, or bonobos, tend to spend only part of their day aloft, though they sleep in tree nests. Common chimps sleep in tree nests, as well, and will climb for food, but spend much of their waking life on their feet and knuckles on the ground. Gorillas, the largest apes, though they climb, in most parts of their range seem to prefer the forest floor.

There is one great ape, however, that spends most of its life in the trees: the orang-utan. It is lighter than a gorilla but heavier than a human, and it seems conscious of its weight. It doesn't scamper like a monkey or swing like a gibbon. Rather, it moves slowly, deliberately and skilfully with all four limbs, almost as if strolling through the foliage.

None of the flat, transparent animals in the oceans are quite as fascinating, or as long, as leptocephali. Eels as a group have one of the most eventful life cycles on the planet, and it all starts with a leptocephalus, ancient Greek for 'slender head'. This refers to the head on the larva of the European eel *Anguilla anguilla* – the best studied of the eels and a source of fascination since Aristotle declared that eels came from earthworms. It wasn't until 1893, though, that anyone made the connection between the European eel and what had been known as *Leptocephalus brevirostris*. And it's no wonder. Who would have thought a 1-2mm (0.04-0.08in), transparently flat, slightly fish-shaped thing in the sea was the same animal as the familiar snaky inhabitant of European fresh water?

This is what biologists believe happens: at about 10–14 years of age, adult eels get the overwhelming urge to swim down river and across the Atlantic to the Sargasso Sea. How and why is a mystery. It's believed that they spawn in the Sargasso (but no one has seen them doing it) and die. The eggs hatch into leptocephali, which drift in the Gulf Stream for three years, finally reaching Europe. Now 4.5cm (1.8in), they metamorphose into elvers and migrate upriver. Years later, as adult eels, they will get the call to make the long, hard journey to the sea to produce another generation of extremely flat leptocephali.

Flattest animal

NAME	**leptocephali**, or **glass eels**, *Anguilla* species
LOCATION	Atlantic and Pacific Oceans
SIZE	elongate and leaf thin

In AD 70, Pliny the Elder, one of the first great natural historians, wrote, 'There is in India a tree whose property it is to plant itself. It spreads out mighty arms to the earth…'. He was writing about adventitious roots, which are the secret of the banyan's reputation as the world's greatest shade-giving tree.

Like many of the nearly 2,000 other species of fig, the banyan can send roots down from its branches. These create pillars that support the branches as they continue to spread. The carefully tended banyan in the Indian Botanic Garden, Calcutta, with its 2,800 prop roots, is the largest known banyan. All over southern Asia, the trees are cared for and used as gathering places – as markets or schools or for village assemblies – and, indeed, the name comes from *banias*, or merchants, because that was where English traders did business with the locals.

Other species of fig famous for their adventitious roots are the 'stranglers', which germinate from seeds in another tree's canopy and send roots coiling down the trunk. Eventually, the fig crushes the host to death, leaving just a tall fig tree in its place. The success of fig trees is partly the result of the adaptability of their roots, but these aren't always adventitious. When growing like normal trees, they take the soil as it comes: thin, and the roots spread out; deep, and they go straight down. The deepest ever recorded are those of a fig in South Africa, measuring 120m (400ft).

Biggest canopy

NAME **banyan tree**, or **barh**, *Ficus benghalensis*
LOCATION southern and South-east Asia
SIZE the largest has a diameter of 420m (1,378ft)

Extreme

Families

Deadliest love life · Strangest incubation · Most agile embryo

Male with the most mates · Flashiest male · Greatest number of spores

Longest continuous incubation · Most artistic suitor · Most sex organs

Tastiest sex · Strangest nuptial gift · Longest lasting love bite · Biggest seed

Greatest mass egg-laying · Largest egg · Shortest mammal gestation

Sexiest immaculate conception · Most fertile animal · Largest nest

Strangest society · Sexiest promotion · Most extreme sex act · Biggest orgy

Most colourful male · Sexiest animal · Most traumatic insemination

Sparkliest animal · Most imaginative use of dung · Oldest juvenile

Most quarrelsome siblings · Greatest sex divide · Longest pregnancy

Strangest nesting material

Deadliest love life

NAME **agile antechinus** *Antechinus agilis*

LOCATION Australia

EVENT every male dies after mating, from stress

This little insect-eating, marsupial mouse has a short but promiscuous life. Like all antechinus species, agile antechinus have a brief, two-week mating season when life becomes supercharged. Being secretive, nocturnal tree-climbers, their mating behaviour in the wild isn't well known, but they are being studied in captivity by biologists keen to understand the effects of reproductive stress.

In July or August, males become flooded with testosterone and other hormones, and that's when the mating frenzy starts. But it's the smaller females who make the running. The males gather together in tree nests, where the females go to look for mates. The females seem to prefer dominant and therefore larger males, but they can't be too fussy, since they mate with several different individuals. A male, too, mates several times. Yet ejaculation goes on for at least three hours, and he stays locked to his mate for up to 12 hours, to make sure his sperm gets to her storage site first.

Alas, the surge of hormones and all the effort is just too much for his immune system. If gastric ulcers and kidney failure from stress don't kill him, infections or parasites do, and he dies within days of his copulation – along with all other males in all the populations. Some females, though, live to mate a second year. They also have the upper hand when it comes to the gender of the next generation, as the sex ratio of their babies (which are kept in a true marsupial pouch) is often skewed towards females.

Strangest incubation

Both these remarkable frogs are probably extinct. The last southern gastric-brooding frog, *Rheobatrachus silus,* was seen in 1981, and the last northern gastric-brooding frog, *R. vitellinus,* in 1985. Strangely, the northern species remained common until March 1985, but was absent three months later and hasn't been seen since. Their extinction is a terrible loss – not just of two exceptional species but also of a whole unique method of incubation and brooding.

As their common name suggests, the frogs would incubate their eggs and then brood their young inside the mother's stomach. They were the only animals in the world known to do such a thing. The female literally swallowed her fertilised eggs, which developed into tadpoles and then froglets inside her stomach. She could not eat during the gestation period of 6–7 weeks and eventually gave birth through her mouth, with one or two fully formed froglets at a time hopping into the outside world. During this remarkable process, the production of the digestive secretion, hydrochloric acid, actually stopped – effectively turning the stomach into a temporary womb.

In both species, the brood size was 20–25, and the whole delivery took about a day and a half. After another four days, the digestive tract returned to normal and the female resumed feeding. Why these frogs became extinct is still unclear, though timber harvesting may have been partly to blame. There have been intensive searches for them since, but to no avail.

NAME	**gastric-brooding** or **platypus frogs**, *Rheobatrachus vitellinus* and *R. silus*
LOCATION	Queensland, Australia
ABILITY	incubating babies in their stomachs

This little baby is a miracle climber. It pops out from its mother's cloaca as a virtual embryo – blind and not much bigger than a broad bean – almost small enough for the mother not to notice she has given birth. Then it has to journey on its own up to the pouch. It has only partially developed forelegs and must drag itself up its mother's fur. Yet surprisingly, it can complete the journey to the pouch in record time – not much longer than about three minutes.

Once it has clamped on to a nipple, it resumes a sort of embryo existence, fattening up on its mother's rich milk, the consistency of which changes as the baby matures and requires different nutrients. It will be as long as four months before the joey releases from the teat, six months before it first leaves the pouch and eight months before it leaves for good. It continues to suckle for another four months by sticking its head into the pouch and, should danger threaten, will also use its mother's enormous pouch as an escape hole.

A female red kangaroo can, in fact, mate and produce a new embryo shortly after giving birth, but this embryo remains dormant until its sibling has left the pouch. It attaches to a vacant, short teat, while its sibling uses the now-longer nipple it has always suckled from. Should anything happen to the joey before it's weaned, the embryo will immediately start maturing – an efficient insurance policy for hard times.

Most agile embryo

NAME	**red kangaroo** *Macropus rufus*
LOCATION	Australia
ABILITY	climbing at least 10–15cm (4–6in) from its mother's cloaca to her pouch

Male mammals are capable of fathering many more offspring than females and so, for some mammals, it makes sense for one male to collect as many females as he can, defend them from other males and then sire as many offspring as possible. This is known as 'polygyny'. The mammal that has taken polygyny the furthest is the male southern elephant seal, a few of which mate with up to 100 females a season (though 40-50 is more usual).

Adult males spend most of the year at sea, then arrive on the breeding beaches in August. The biggest ones claim territories where they know females will come ashore, in September and early October, to have the pups they conceived a year earlier. When the females have given birth, they go into oestrus, and the dominant males mate with as many as possible in order to have the maximum number of offspring the following year.

Of course a few males with lots of mates means lots of males with no mates at all, and for every breeding colony, there's a huge adjacent bachelor colony full of disgruntled seals with little better to do than sneak over and try to mate with the females next door. What distinguishes the southern elephant seal from the northern elephant seal in the North Pacific, which has a similar mating system, is that northern bachelors are more successful at sneaky mating, making their southern relatives the current record-holders for the most polygynous mammal.

Male with the most mates

NAME	**southern elephant seal** *Mirounga leonina*
LOCATION	subantarctic islands and southern Argentina
ABILITY	mating with more females than any other male mammal

Flashiest male

NAME **morpho butterflies** *Morpho* species
LOCATION Central and South American rainforests
ABILITY producing vivid flashes with the most iridescent of living structures

Of all the butterflies, the iridescent blue morphos have always been the most sought after by collectors, their wings even used for jewellery. The males' vivid colour flashes, visible even from aircraft flying over the rainforest canopy, are not for wooing females, however. The iridescence is in fact for intimidating rivals and claiming territory.

Such intense colour is produced not by pigments but by possibly the most complicated reflective structures in the world. The wing scales (the 'powder' that rubs off a wing) are angled like roof tiles. Each scale supports another series of layered, near-transparent scales, which may be topped by further structures. The purpose is to reflect light not just upwards but also outwards. The structures are so precisely arranged that light rays of a particular wavelength are reflected back in the same but parallel direction, enhancing each other and therefore the reflected colour. Result: extreme vivid colour.

Being so flashy is dangerous, however (females, by comparison, are camouflage brown). So the males have another trick. When they fly, the movement of their wings up and down alters the angle of light striking the scales and the colour changes suddenly from bright blue to brown. The effect, enhanced by an undulating, chaotic flight and the exposure in the upward stroke of brown underwings, is that the butterfly appears and disappears. And as soon as it settles and closes its wings, exposing just the brown undersurface, it melts into the forest.

Greatest number of spores

Most large fungi spread themselves by releasing into the air multitudes of microscopic spores from special fruiting bodies – mushrooms and toadstools – that grow above ground. Some use animals, water or even plants to help move the spores, but most rely on the wind to blow them away, sometimes over huge distances. The spores are usually released by the use of special turgid cells, which means that most fruiting bodies can't risk drying out. These mushrooms and toadstools therefore usually grow when it's damp.

The giant puffball, however, doesn't rain spores from a multitude of downward-facing pores or gills in the usual way. Instead, it bears them internally, keeping them nicely humid, and releases them gradually. If conditions are moist enough, it matures in just a week or so, swelling to huge proportions– sometimes to more than a metre. It then begins to split open, aided by the odd animal knock and abrasion, to release over weeks or even months billions or trillions of spores into the wind. This isn't considered a very efficient method of dispersal, as most spores will neither travel far nor survive, which is why it produces so many of them. But then the job is done if just a few spores settle and 'germinate' in favorable (nitrogen-rich) nearby pastures. It's also a good thing that all the spores don't grow into puffballs. If they did, in just a couple of generations, the puffballs would have a total volume many times that of the Earth.

NAME	**giant puffball** *Calvatia gigantea*
LOCATION	temperate regions
ABILITY	producing up to 20 trillion spores from just one fruiting body

Longest continuous incubation

NAME **emperor penguin** *Aptenodytes forsteri*

LOCATION Antarctica

ABILITY incubating its egg through the worst of the Antarctic winter

This is the largest of the 17 species of penguin and the only one that incubates through the Antarctic winter. Other birds such as kiwis (see p.278) have longer incubation periods, but they share duties and leave their nests to feed. The male emperor penguin, though, sits on an egg for the entire time it takes to hatch: 62–67 days.

It all starts in late March or early April on the Antarctic sea ice where, after a summer feeding at sea, tens of thousands of the penguins gather to court and mate. By the time the eggs are laid, about 50 days have passed – and the penguins have had nothing to eat. Then, as the females all start walking back to the sea – which, because of the steadily growing sea ice, is farther away than it used to be – each male holds his egg on top of his feet and covers it with his brood pouch, a feathery flap of skin. The males stand huddled together through the depths of the Antarctic winter. It's dark or semi-dark, gales blow, blizzards rage and temperatures may drop to –40° C (–40° F), not counting the wind-chill factor.

Two months pass, the eggs hatch, the chicks stay under the brood pouch, and in a few days the females start turning up. It's been about 120 days since the males have eaten anything other than snow, but they're finally free to go fishing. There's just one problem – the sea now can be as far as 100 km (62 miles) away.

Most artistic suitor

This little bird creates true works of art, each a unique display. Instead of wearing colourful plumage, the male Vogelkop bowerbird courts females by appealing to their sense of aesthetics – a sort of sexual selection through art. Even more extraordinary, different populations have developed different cultural styles.

In the Arfak, Tamrau and Wandamen Mountains, a male starts with a 'maypole' – a forest sapling – around which he weaves a conical stick hut up to 1.2m (4ft) high and 1.8m (6ft) wide, with an arch for an entrance. Outside he lays a huge carpet of green moss on which he arranges, according to colour and size, his treasures – thousands of them, from berries and flowers to butterfly and beetle wings. Such an elaborate construction using fresh material needs constant renovation and guarding from other males, which can lead to almost year-round drudgery, but at least he has the safety of drab female colours instead of extravagant plumage. The more impressive the size and colourfulness of his bower, the more females will allow him to mate with them.

In the Kumawa and Fakfak Mountains, however, females have developed a different artistic taste, perhaps determined by the local availability of objects for decoration. Here the males build dowdy towers decorated with dull objects such as snail shells and stones. It may be that, in years to come, selection of males for the artistic merits of their bowers – effectively, symbolic sexual symbols – will lead to one species, divided by mountains, becoming two.

NAME **Vogelkop bowerbird**, or **brown gardener**, *Amblyornis inornatus*
LOCATION Irian Jaya, Indonesian New Guinea
ABILITY building the most elaborately decorated structure created by a non-human animal

Most sex organs

NAME **tapeworm** *Polygonoporus giganticus*
LOCATION the gut
SIZE depends on the size of the gut

Tapeworms are truly remarkable beasts that have been with us, intimately, since we were proto-humans. Since they mainly inhabit guts of animals, it follows that the biggest guts are likely to have the biggest worms. Imagine, then, the excitement of a parasitologist presented with the challenge of dissecting the gut of a huge whale. Each type of tapeworm comprises a grappling head-like region (but one with no mouth, eyes or brain), designed primarily to attach to the gut of its host, followed by a sort of a neck, which is the production line for the segments that make up the body.

Each segment is a self-contained reproduction kit, with testes and ovaries, able to absorb nutrients from juices in its host's gut. In the case of probably the longest tapeworm in the world, *Polygonoporus giganticus*, which lives in sperm whales, the body is reputed to be up to 40m (131ft) long with up to 45,000 segments. Since each segment has 4–14 sets of genitalia, that means a possible 630,000 sex organs. Its eggs are shed continually, millions a day. Luckily for their hosts, bigger tapeworms seem to be confined to one per gut. And since some tapeworms self-fertilise, there may be no problem about getting to meet a mate. It's lucky for us, though, that the adult phase of *Diphyllobothrium latum*, the largest tapeworm infecting humans (about 10 million of us), seldom gets to be longer than 10m (33ft). Or is it really so lucky to have a 10m long tapeworm inside you?

Tastiest sex

Mating is a problem for most male spiders, as females are usually larger and extremely predatory. A male must therefore let his prospective mate know that her visitor comes bearing sperm, quite literally: he collects sperm from his genitals in each of his two pedipalps (the leg-like appendages either side of his mouth). These sexual 'arms' have bulb-like ends that fit, in lock-and-key fashion, into the genitalia of the female of his species.

Some males merely do a dance, make an appropriate signal, or offer a food parcel to earn enough time to mate. But those with short lifespans, and therefore the prospect of mating only once, may have to sacrifice their lives to make sure that only their sperm fertilises the female. When a male Australian red-back spider inserts his first palp into the female, he somersaults over her so his abdomen is directly over her mouth-parts, presenting her with the opportunity to eat him. In an average 65 per cent of matings, the male really is eaten, often when the female is underweight. But this, the ultimate sacrifice, allows him long enough to insert all his sperm.

The black-and-yellow garden spider male goes one step further: he dies immediately after inserting his second palp, which swells up inside the female. Neither males queuing up to mate nor the female herself can dislodge his palp, at least not for a quarter of an hour or so, by which time his sperm has done its job. And of course, the most productive way for a female to dislodge the body hanging from her is to eat it.

NAME **black-and-yellow garden spider**
Argiope aurantia

LOCATION North and Central America

EVENT the male dies during sex and the female then eats him

Strangest nuptial gift

If you were about to give a female one fifth of your body weight in sperm and nutrients, you'd want to make sure she didn't die before her eggs were fertilised and deposited. And if her biggest danger was being eaten by a spider, you'd want to do something to prevent that happening. This is how the scarlet-bodied wasp moth does it. He visits a plant such as dog fennel and feeds on the poison (pyrrolizidine alkaloids) that it contains. The chemicals, which affect spiders and most other invertebrates, then make their way to the moth's pair of abdominal pouches, which are packed with fine, absorbent filaments. The male finds a female and, as part of his courtship, festoons her with these sticky, alkaloid-laden filaments. And just to make sure she is protected, he also injects some of the alkaloid along with his sperm.

The dog fennel produces pyrrolizidine alkaloids to keep its leaves from being eaten by insect herbivores, but nature always seems to find a way around things – and, indeed, the scarlet-bodied wasp moth has evolved an immunity to the poison. Spiders can detect the alkaloids when they examine a catch, and none of them wants even to touch a female scarlet-bodied wasp moth, much less eat her. Biologists proved this by putting a filament-festooned female on a spider's web: the spider cut away the strands of web that were holding her and released her, alive. This is the only known instance of a male insect making his mate invulnerable in such a way.

NAME	**scarlet-bodied wasp moth**
	Cosmosoma myrodora
LOCATION	American tropics and sub-tropics
ABILITY	the male makes the female invulnerable to spider attacks

Longest lasting love bite

In the 1830s, when scientists first became aware of this strange suborder of fishes and started trawling specimens up from the depths – between 300m (980ft) and 4,000m (13,000ft) – there seemed to be some species that were represented entirely by females. Then someone examined a tumour-like growth that a few of these females seemed to have and was shocked to discover the male. He had fused on to her body, losing the ability to do anything independently. Even her circulatory system had extended into his body.

Since then a lot has been learned about some of the most extreme instances of sexual dimorphism (physical difference between the sexes – see p310) in these fishes. The male is generally less than a tenth of the female's size. In one of the largest species, *Ceratias holboelli*, for example, he measures 7.3cm (2.8in), and she's a whopping 77cm (30.3in).

The male starts life near the surface as a tiny larva, metamorphoses into an adult and then descends to a world that's dark and vast. He has to find a female of his species when there are probably only a handful of them in a cubic kilometre. Fortunately, he's equipped with big nostrils, a big mouth, a pair of pincer-like teeth, one of the best senses of smell and proportionately big eyes to look for the bioluminescent lure a female uses to attract prey. If he's lucky, he finds a female, bites and holds on. Then his eyes, nostrils – everything but testicles – degenerate. And he's left with one simple role in life – to fertilise eggs.

NAME	**deep-sea anglerfishes** Ceratioidei family
LOCATION	ocean depths
ABILITY	sexual parasitism

These so-called double coconuts were impressing people long before the islands they came from were ever discovered. They used to wash up on beaches around the Indian Ocean, and sailors would pick them up at sea. Before the discovery of the Seychelles in 1743, the general belief was that they were the fruit of a gigantic tree growing on the ocean floor – hence coco-de-mer or 'nut-of-the-sea'. Then, for a time, they were thought to come from the Maldives, which accounts for the scientific species name. Another theory was that they were from the Tree of Knowledge in the Garden of Eden, and the reason for that one is pretty obvious: the striking resemblance to a woman from waist to mid-thigh. Naturally, they were also thought to be aphrodisiacs.

The reality is pretty fantastic, too. The coco-de-mer palm is incredibly slow growing. The first leaf starts to appear nine months after germination begins, and the first flower can take another 60 years (there are male and female palms). The two-lobed fruit may take up to ten years to ripen, and it may be a century before the tree reaches its full growth of about 30m (100ft). The tree's leaves, when they've finally grown, can be 6m (20ft) long. As for the nuts, they are edible and are a lot like coconut. It's not likely, though, that anyone would be eating them nowadays. The tree is close to extinction, and the nuts, which are sometimes sold to botanical gardens, can cost as much as £800 ($1,500) each.

Biggest seed

NAME	**coco-de-mer**, or **Seychelles nut**, *Lodoicea maldivica*
LOCATION	Praslin and Curicusc islands, Seychelles
SIZE	the fruit can be up to 48cm (19in) across and weigh more than 22kg (48lb)

Greatest mass egg-laying

NAME   **olive ridley turtle** *Lepidochelys oliveacea*
LOCATION   sandy beaches on the coast of Orissa, north-east India
EVENT   500,000 or more turtles may arrive to lay their eggs

At any time from December to March, a huge flotilla of female olive ridley turtles arrives in the Bay of Bengal for an orgy of egg-laying. This mass arrival has happened almost every year for thousands – possibly millions – of years, and the river-delta beaches used comprise the biggest turtle rookery in the world. The largest recorded arrival there, in 1991, involved 610,000 olive ridleys.

The turtles travel possibly thousands of kilometres from their feeding grounds, mate offshore where the males congregate, and then haul themselves up the beaches at night to nest. They may even return a few weeks later to lay more eggs. Each one buries an average 100–150 soft-shelled eggs in the sand. If the eggs are not eaten by predators such as dogs and crows or washed away by beach erosion, they will hatch in about 45 days, and the babies will dig themselves out at night and run to the sea. But only one in a thousand will make it back to its birth-beach as an adult.

In the past 14 years, more than 120,000 olive ridleys are estimated to have drowned in the nets of trawlers fishing illegally within 10–20km (6.2–12.4 miles) of the coast during the nesting season. The area is also being developed, and there is a plan for a huge port complex close to one of the key breeding beaches. Conservationists worldwide are now pressing the state and national government to make sure that this, one of the greatest of the world's wildlife spectacles, gets the protection it deserves.

The biggest egg actually belongs to the ostrich, weighing in at
1–17.8 kg (2.2–39 lb). But it's only about 1 per cent of the
bird's weight. The largest eggs relative to body size and
weight belong to storm petrels, hummingbirds and kiwis.
The brown kiwi produces an egg so large in relation to its
hen-sized body cavity that an x-ray of its body appears
almost all egg. Though the egg is two thirds yoke and weighs
up to 15–17 per cent of its mother, it's laid after just 34 days –
one of the fastest gestations of any bird.

Not surprisingly, a kiwi usually lays only 2–3 eggs a year.
Incubation, though, is one of the longest of any bird, taking
up to 84 days, and is shared by the male (kiwis pair for life).
When the mini-kiwi breaks out of its egg, it is fully feathered
and has a kick-start ration of yoke in its stomach. This
almost mammal-like birth isn't surprising for a bird that has
the lifestyle of a mammal. The kiwi is flightless with fur-like
feathers, nocturnal, lives in a burrow, has unbird-like senses
of hearing and smell (for locating food), cat-like whiskers and
a body-temperature of 38°C (100°F), which is 2°C less than
that of most birds. But the true origin of the enormous baby
could be the kiwi's ancestry. It's a descendant of a lineage of
giant birds that also gave rise to emus, and though its body is
dwarf-sized by comparison, it's kept a virtually emu-sized egg.

Largest egg

NAME **brown kiwi** *Apteryx australis*

LOCATION New Zealand

SIZE up to 450 g (1 lb), filling up to 25 per cent of
its mother's body

Shortest mammal gestation

NAME	**stripe-faced dunnart** *Sminthopsis macroura*
LOCATION	Australia
TIME	9.5–11 days

Dunnarts are marsupial mammals. Like all marsupials, they produce tiny, undeveloped babies – embryos, almost – after a very short gestation period, or pregnancy. In fact, these newborns are so undeveloped that, at first, they breathe through their skin. Many marsupials have extremely short gestation periods, and just 12–13 days is common in a number of species, including the American opossum and the long-nosed bandicoot. But the stripe-faced dunnart has the shortest gestation of all: as the breeding season progresses, it can shorten to just 9.5 days.

Like other mammals, marsupial embryos initially get all their nutrition while in the womb from their mother's blood (via a placenta – an exchange organ). But while other mammalian babies remain in the womb for much longer, marsupials continue their development in their mother's external, abdominal pouch. And instead of receiving nutrition from their mother's blood, they fatten up on her milk. Not surprisingly, marsupials often produce milk for much longer than other mammals. The striped-faced dunnart continues to supply milk for more than two months – enough to feed as many as eight babies (she can produce more, but as she has just eight nipples, the excess babies will die). She carries her brood in her pouch as she scampers around after insects - until they get too big and must hitch a ride piggy-back style should danger threaten.

Though not the most colourful of lizards, whiptails are the most genetically challenging. It took more than 100 years for biologists to realise that, in the Chihuahuan spotted whiptail and other species, no males existed. The all-female species were reproducing by 'parthenogenesis' – without fertilisation. It's now known that, among the higher animals, some other lizards, a few salamanders, the Brahminy blind snake and a number of fish can also clone themselves. And individual snakes and domestic chickens and turkeys occasionally produce fertile eggs without sex, though the offspring are male and don't have all of their mother's genes.

Of the other species of whiptails that are parthenogenic, about half are triploid like the Chihuahuan whiptail, containing three sets of chromosomes. (Most animals are diploid, having only two sets: one coming from the mother and the other from the father.) Biologists guess the triploid state resulted from two whiptail species crossing and their hybrid offspring then crossing with another whiptail. Strangely, one hangover of their past sexual lives remains: they can't give birth unless they pretend to mate, one female taking the role of a male. Biologists think that doing away with sex allowed them to reproduce themselves faster than their sexual relatives and so spread far and wide rapidly – a good short-term strategy. In the long term, though, should conditions change dramatically, the theory says that these little clones may not have the genetic diversity to enable them to adapt and survive. But this could just prove to be sexual bias.

Sexiest immaculate conception

NAME	**Chihuahuan spotted whiptail**
	Cnemidophorus exsanguis
LOCATION	south-western USA and Mexico
ABILITY	virgin birth

Most fertile animal

NAME   **aphids** Aphididae family

HABIT   plant suckers

ABILITY   a female is capable of giving rise to a billion clones in a year

For most of her life, a female aphid produces identical copies of herself without sex. On average, she can do so every ten days, and since these clones are themselves pregnant before they are born, with their embryos containing embryos, a billion-fold increase in an aphid population is theoretically possible in just a year.

Aphids have been around since plants first appeared on Earth. They are bugs with needle-like mouthparts for sucking up plant sap. If the sap is rich in nitrogen, say, from artificial fertilisers, they grow even faster. Some act as cows for ants, which milk them for their honeydew excretions. In return, the ants guard them and may even build shelters for them, store their eggs in winter or move them to new plants. These aphid populations may reproduce even more successfully, presumably because they are relatively free from insect predators such as ladybird, lacewing and hoverfly larvae.

If the population gets too great for the host plant or the plant begins to die, they may start to give birth to winged progeny, and thus they can then spread themselves to pastures new, making use of the wind. These winged individuals may produce sexual offspring on a new host species, the females of which lay eggs. But the size of a population is relative to the food supply, which in temperate areas declines as winter approaches. And in a healthy environment, the predator numbers are in tune with the cycles of their prey. So a rain of aphids is merely the stuff of nightmares.

The largest *tree* nest ever recorded was built in Florida by bald eagles. It had probably been added to over the years and was 2.9m (9.4ft) wide and 6m (20ft) deep. More normal bald eagle nests are much smaller – mere stick piles compared to nests made by the true nest-building record-holder.

However, a group of birds found in Australasia, called megapodes, use specially prepared incubation mounds to incubate their eggs. The average mound size of the chicken-like orange-footed megapode is about 3.5m (11.5ft) wide and 12m (39ft) high. The male and female, which usually pair for life, build it of soil and organic material.

The effort of constructing a mound, using hundreds of tonnes of small rocks, wood, soil, branches and leaf litter, is immense and requires large and powerful feet – megapode means 'big foot'. A mound may be used over years by many generations, growing larger and larger in the process – the record-beating 50m (164ft) wide specimen could have been in use for hundreds of years. The sun heats the mound, but more importantly, decaying vegetation generates heat, and the temperature inside will be about 25–35°C (77–95°F). While the female lays her eggs – over a period of months – the male continues to tend the mound, adding or removing nest material to regulate the heat. It's rather like a giant, earthy compost heap, and, as the eggs hatch, the young must dig themselves out of the mound unaided.

Largest nest

NAME	**orange-footed megapode**, or **scrubfowl**, *Megapodius reinwardt*
LOCATION	South-east Asia, New Guinea and northern Australia
SIZE	up to 50m (164ft) wide and 4.5m (14.8ft) high

Strangest society

Naked mole rats organise themselves into the largest underground colonies (at least 75–80 individuals and up to 300) of any mammal. Conditions are hard, literally, and hot and humid, and so they have dispensed with fur and normal mammalian temperature control. The younger workers form the digging teams at the earth face searching for food, using their huge front teeth to gnaw the hard soil until they find roots and tubers; they get rid of the soil by reversing along the tunnel and kicking it back up to the surface. A hierarchy exists, and when a subordinate meets a superior in a tunnel, she or he crouches so the other can squeeze over. And like ants, there are guards – older, larger individuals.

Ruling all is the queen – one of the older animals (mole rats can live for 25 years or more), who fought for her position when the previous queen died. Like an ant queen, her abdomen has become elongated, enough to house up to 28 babies. She runs a small harem of males and constantly bullies the rest of the colony so that all are too stressed to reproduce. There's sense in such organisation. Where naked mole rats live, rain is unpredictable, and so there is no set season for reproduction. But underground, where there are always tubers to eat so long as there is a team to dig for them, it makes sense to have a social system where a colony behaves like one big organism, allowing a queen to breed all year round.

Clownfish are probably best known for their immunity to the stinging tentacles of sea anemones and the fact that particular fish live their whole lives among the tentacles of particular anemones. But it gets even more specific than that. Only a maximum of six clownfish will occupy one anemone, and only two of those will breed. The other four just reside there, tolerated by the breeding pair as long as they keep their places in the very strict clownfish hierarchy.

The dominant fish, and the largest, is the breeding female. Number two is the smaller breeding male, three is the next biggest, and so on. The fish control their own growth, and each fish in the pecking order is no more than 80 per cent of the size of the one just above it. Any fish that gets uppity by growing larger than its allotted size is evicted from the home anemone to open water and, without any tentacles for protection (all the other appropriate anemones are usually occupied), to almost certain death.

So clownfish are very careful about their growth, and since they're long-lived, the little societies can survive without disturbance for tens of years. But when a fish does die, every fish below it is promoted and grows a little, and a new juvenile is allowed in. What happens, though, when the breeding female dies? Who takes her place? The breeding male, of course. Anything that can control its size can, it seems, control its sex, and so he turns himself into a her.

Sexiest promotion

NAME   **clown anemonefish** *Amphiprion percula*
LOCATION   southern and western Pacific reefs
EVENT   males get promoted and become female

Most extreme sex act

NAME   **slender banana slug** *Ariolimax dolichophallus*

LOCATION   California

EVENT   one partner may gnaw off the other's penis

This is probably the most famous of slugs. It is not only beautiful, for a slug, but it is also the official mascot of the University of California, Santa Cruz. The species is granted such respect in part for its exclusivity – it is found only in the redwood forests of central coastal California – but mainly for its intriguing sexual behaviour. Rumours exist that the slender banana slug has the world's longest penis relative to body size, but that record is held by a goose barnacle. The penis, nevertheless, is sometimes as long as the slug's entire body (up to 18cm/7in) and the name *dolichophallus* does, indeed, mean 'long penis'.

The banana slug, like other slugs and snails, has both a female opening and a penis. After a long and sensual courtship two slugs copulate on a bed of slime, each as both a male and a female simultaneously, for many hours at a time. But sometimes the female reproductive tract grips the penis so tightly that it can't be withdrawn. The only thing the one entrapped slug can do is the act of apophally: gnaw off its penis (often helped by its partner). The plus side is that this prevents the castrated slug wasting resources on providing other slugs with sperm, and so, the theory goes, it will divert more energy into growing its fertilised eggs. And, of course, its partner will have had a nutritious, post-coital snack.

Biggest orgy

Corals have devised a spectacular way to maximise their chances of cross-fertilising: the mass release of sperm and eggs. The most dramatic of these procreation events occurs on the Great Barrier Reef – the largest coral reef ecosystem in the world. Mass spawning of reefs in the area occurs over a few nights after a full moon, in October, November or sometimes December, and involves more than 140 different coral species. This spectacular phenomenon is synchronised by three main environmental cues: warming of the seawater in spring, which triggers the eggs and sperm to mature (most corals are hermaphrodites), the lunar cycle (peak spawning is 4-6 nights after a full moon) and darkness.

The mass spawning creates a pink and white underwater snowstorm, as billions of coral polyps release their small egg-and-sperm bundles. These float to the surface, where the sperm fertilise the eggs. The fish have a bonanza, but there are only so many eggs they can eat, and some eggs contain deterrent chemicals. Within hours of fertilisation, an egg develops into an embryo, which becomes a small larva and floats away searching for a free place on the seabed to settle and start a coral colony through multiplication of itself. Mass coral spawning is one of the world's great wonders, repeated by some but not all coral reefs around the world. The slick formed by the eggs on the surface can be seen from space; surprisingly, though, the event was recorded for the first time only in 1981.

NAME	**reef corals** - more than 140 species
LOCATION	Great Barrier Reef, Australia
EVENT	sperm and eggs are released by all the corals at the same time on the same night

Most colourful male

NAME   **sapphire copepods** *Sapphirina* species

LOCATION   sub-tropical and tropical oceans

ABILITY   glittering with the most beautiful iridescence

Sapphire copepods are millimetre-sized, woodlouse-shaped crustaceans (small relations of shrimps and crabs) and form part of the sea's rich plankton. Colour plays a critically important role in their lives. While the free-swimming female stays as inconspicuous as she can, the rather more sedentary, iridescent-blue male literally sparkles – reflecting a rainbow of colours whenever the sun strikes him. His body covering, or cuticle, contains layer after layer of crystal platelets that act like prisms, and the iridescence comes from the diffraction and refraction of white light as it shines through them.

Intriguingly, different males – even though they belong to the same *Sapphirina* species – have prismatic crystals of different thickness that produce different colours. Why, though, no one knows for sure. The males are not free-swimming but live inside transparent salps (jet-propelled, barrel-shaped animals), eating away at their insides, and are dependent on the salps for transport. The likelihood is that the parasitic males have to flash to signal their whereabouts to the females. Indeed, their potential mates have far better developed eyes than they do and can see in 3D, presumably to help them locate flashing males.

Once a female finds a suitably colourful flasher and indicates that she likes him, he swims out of his salp and they mate. But the downside for the male is that his host may have since moved on, and so he is left homeless and with no food supply until he can find another likely looking salp to sneak up to and into.

Sexiest animal

NAME **bonobo**, or **pygmy chimpanzees**
Pan paniscus

LOCATION Democratic Republic of Congo,
south of the Congo River

ABILITY uses creative sex to build relationships
and make peace

For bonobos, sex is neither taboo nor merely a method of reproduction. It's an essential part of social intercourse. Erotic contact between individuals, of whatever gender or age, is used to avoid conflict, make peace and create a harmonious society. Proper sex is comparatively casual and quick but, as with humans, it's often conducted face to face, with partners looking into each other's eyes. Erotic contact between females is common. Genital rubbing and grooming maintains close friendships and also enables young females migrating to a new group (males stay in the group they were born into) to bond with established females. In fact, bonobo society – unlike chimpanzee society – is female centred, and female friends will join forces to keep aggressive males under control. Males don't form such close bonds, but even they may calm or appease each other by pretend copulation or by rubbing bottoms or even penises. The closest relationship for a male is with his mother, whom he remains attached to throughout her life. His status depends on hers.

Bonobos resemble humans by occasionally walking upright (though they spend much of their lives in the trees) and displaying great intelligence – in captivity, they can even communicate using basic human language. But with the help of sex, easing tension, their peaceable culture places them apart from both humans and common chimpanzees.

Females usually become pregnant only every 6–7 years, and youngsters are nursed until at least five years old. But in today's war-torn, human-dominated world, such slow reproduction is disastrous for bonobos. Logging of their rainforest home and rampant poaching has fragmented their population and may have reduced numbers to fewer than 10,000 individuals.

Most traumatic insemination

NAME	**common bedbug** *Cimex lectularius*
LOCATION	possibly in a bed near you
EVENT	the male stabs the female to inject his sperm

A male bedbug not only has mouth-parts for sucking up human blood but also a sperm-delivery needle (an evolved penis) for stabbing female bedbugs. Sperm is injected directly into the female's blood and swims up to her ovaries. Unfortunately, though, the stab wounds may let in infection. This rather violent technique has evolved as a way of bypassing the female's genital passage and therefore any control she has over the timing of conception, as well as any anti-sperm devices. (Female animals are believed to have such devices, since if a male isn't staying around to help with child-rearing, a female may prefer to widen the genetic options by mating with several males, even selecting whose sperm to use to father her offspring.)

'Traumatic extragenital insemination' seems an extreme example of males getting on top in the sexual-conflict arms race. But females have evolved a counter-action. Judging by the scars on a female, a copulating male's body position often results in his organ piercing in the region of her fifth segment. If he stabs to the right, his organ slides into a notch that directs it into a kind of holding pocket, complete with spermicidal cells that can kill both unwanted sperm and microbes. Females mated in this way live longer and produce more eggs. A male, though, is on the watch for promiscuous females. He has taste sensors on his stabbing organ, and if these detect sperm, he injects far fewer of his own, saving his resources for his real desire: virgins.

Sparkliest animal

At night from March to May, Toyama Bay on the west coast of the Japanese island of Honshu lights up. The water flashes, sparkles, shimmers and glows, and the spectacle attracts visitors from all over Japan and from around the world. Toyama prefecture has even declared the bay a Special Natural Monument. What happens there is the annual spawning of the firefly squid. There are hundreds of thousands of small squid, each 4–6cm (1.6–2.4in) long, capable of producing light from hundreds of special light-producing patches of tissue on their skin called photophores. Animals that produce light are called bioluminescent, and Japanese firefly squid are probably the most exuberantly bioluminescent creatures on the planet.

When they're spawning (producing eggs and sperm), the squid are undoubtedly using their lighting as a form of sexual communication, but when they're not spawning, they have other uses for it.

They spend most of the year out in the open sea, either in the Pacific or the Sea of Japan. During the day they stay at a depth of 200–600m (650–1,970ft), and at night they rise to the surface. It's thought that they use the photophores to break up their outlines, confuse predators and possibly even lure in prey. Cephalopods (squid, octopus, cuttlefish) are very visual animals, but the firefly squid, which probably can see in colour, may be the most visual of all.

NAME	**Japanese firefly squid** *Watasenia scintillans*
LOCATION	western Pacific
ABILITY	putting on a mass underwater display of bioluminescence

Most imaginative use of dung

NAME   **burrowing owl** *Athene cunicularia*

LOCATION   grasslands of North, Central and South America

ABILITY   using dung as bait to catch beetles

A burrowing owl uses a burrow as shelter, to rest, hide and nest in. Its scientific name *cunicularia* means 'little miner', but it likes a ready-made burrow best. Come spring, a male burrowing owl will select or dig a burrow – ideally in short-grass habitat with insects and small rodents that can be seen easily and caught at ground level. It may then collect dung – especially shredded cow or horse dung (in times past, it might have been buffalo or antelope dung) – and place it inside the nest chamber and around the entrance.

It has been suggested that this might mask the smell of the eggs and young to protect them from predators such as American badgers. But a more nutritious use has been discovered. The regurgitated pellets of owls with dung in their burrows contain ten times more dung beetles than those of owls that don't use dung. So the dung beetles, whose own nest activity involves finding dung to roll into balls on which to lay their eggs, are almost certainly being lured by the male owls.

The dung provides meals-on-wheels for the incubating females and, indeed, for the males themselves, who spend much of their time guarding the nest burrows and so have relatively little opportunity to hunt. To date, the only other records of animal use of dung for non-food purposes are as fuel by humans and as nest lining by a bird or two, leaving owls as the record-holders for ingenuity with dung.

Oldest juvenile

NAME **olm**, **human fish**, or **blind cave salamander**, *Proteus anguinus*

LOCATION underground streams in limestone caves in mountains along the Adriatic, from Trieste in Italy to Montenegro

ABILITY existing in a juvenile form for more than 50 years

A 'neotenic' lifestyle – remaining an eternal tadpole, complete with gills and fins – suits a group of salamander-type amphibians that have chosen a near-total aquatic life. In the case of the Mexican axolotl, found in the wild only in two lakes, transformation into a proper land-roaming salamander can occur if the water dries up. But the rest of the neotenic amphibians (including North American mudpuppies and sirens) stay as juveniles for life.

One of the strangest is the eel-like olm, which is blind, has tiny limbs and translucent, baby-pink skin (though a black population exists in Slovenia). It lives in dark, underground caves and hunts insect larvae and other small creatures by smell and vibrations. Being blind isn't a problem,

as it smells it way around and can probably navigate using the earth's magnetic field. When times are hard, it can go without food for years, probably in a state of torpor.

Though it keeps its larval fin and gills throughout life (rumoured to be up to 100 years), when it gets to be seven or so, it becomes sexually mature. The female normally lays eggs, but under certain, perhaps dry, conditions, she is believed to give birth to live young. Biologists think the olm took to a subterranean life after the last ice age, retreating to water in limestone karst formations. Since it never surfaced again, it didn't bother to lose its tadpole fins and gills and so remains an eternal juvenile.

Most quarrelsome siblings

NAME **spotted hyaena cubs** *Crocuta crocuta*

LOCATION African savannah

ABILITY siblings start fighting as soon as they are born

It's tough in the natural world, and even siblings cannot always rely on one another. The first-hatched pups of sand tiger sharks, for instance, quickly use up the food in their yolk sacs and start dining on their smaller brothers and sisters until there are just two dominant pups left, one in each uterus. Spotted hyaena cubs don't actually eat one another, but they start fighting – often quite viciously – the moment they are born.

There are usually two cubs in a litter, and both have very sharp teeth. One often dies of starvation or battle-induced injuries, especially if they are the same sex, but if they are different sexes, they usually both survive. They're not actually fighting over milk (though if the weaker one survives, it accepts that it is subordinate and allows its litter-mate to exclude it from nursing) but are preparing for adult life.

Their success in hunting big animals is largely a result of clan cooperation, but when it comes to feeding on the kill, spotted hyaenas compete vigorously. How much an individual can eat is determined by where it is in the dominance hierarchy. Females are dominant over all the males, and then there is a hierarchy within each sex. Critically, in the case of cubs whose mothers are low-ranking, the amount of food they are allowed to eat determines to a great extent on whether they will survive beyond adolescence. Sibling rivalry is therefore a matter of life or death in more ways than one.

Males and females inevitably have different mating needs and strategies, and that can give them different shapes, colours or sizes. This is known as sexual dimorphism, and it's common throughout the animal kingdom. In the case of most dimorphic animals, the two sexes are enough alike to be recognisable at least as the same species. However, it would be hard to know, just by looking, that a male and female blanket octopus had the remotest connection with each other. The female can be 2m (6.6ft) long and weigh 10kg (22lb). The male grows to all of 2.4cm (0.9in) and nearly 300g (8.8oz). And the reason, essentially, is that they inhabit the open sea, a boundless world controlled by currents.

For the female, this means being as large as possible so that she can produce as many eggs as possible, increasing the chances that at least a few will survive without being eaten. For the male, growing too big would be pointless. All he needs to do is manufacture sperm and focus on searching the ocean for a female. If he finds one – a very big if – he inserts an arm into her gill cavity, and the arm fills with sperm and breaks off. He leaves it there and, having completed his life's mission, floats off and dies. In fact, scientists had only ever seen dead male blanket octopuses until 2003, when the first living one ever seen was caught in the beam of a torch.

Greatest sex divide

NAME   **blanket octopus** *Tremoctopus violaceus*

LOCATION warm seas worldwide

SIZE   the female is 100 times larger than the male

No mother carries eggs or babies longer than she needs to, but the alpine salamander does it for up to three years and two months – the longest gestation recorded for any vertebrate (animal with a backbone). The salamander's average pregnancy is two years – considerably longer than the 20–22-month gestation of an Asiatic elephant – and yet, surprisingly, the female is no more than 14cm (5.6in) long. So why does she do it? The clue is in the alpine location: damp but cold, with only a short period in the spring and summer when she can be active. In fact, the higher she lives, the longer her pregnancy. The likelihood is that, as the altitude increases, it gets more and more difficult for her to find enough food to sustain herself *and* grow babies in just one season.

Strangely, unlike most other amphibians, she doesn't lay eggs. Instead, she nurtures her young internally, in her two oviducts (only mammals have a uterus). She produces 20 or more eggs in each oviduct, but only one egg develops in each – the others provide food for the two growing larvae. Even stranger, the youngsters have special teeth to scrape their mother's reproductive tract, giving them enough nourishment to last their long gestation and to metamorphose from larvae into fully formed salamanders before birth. Once they are born, though, their mother's work is done, and they are left to fend for themselves.

Longest pregnancy

NAME	**alpine salamander** *Salamandra atra*
LOCATION	high mountain forest of alpine regions of Europe
TIME	up to 38 months

Strangest nesting material

A nest functions to keep the eggs together and to cushion, insulate, shelter or conceal them, and nest building is as varied as a bird's ingenuity and the sites and material available. Even the most conservative nest may contain something unusual if nature (or humanity) provides. Common waxbills put carnivore droppings in their nests, possibly as defence against predators. Some wrens and flycatchers use the cast skins of snakes and lizards, and in their absence, they'll collect plastic or cellophane. For other species, if mud isn't available for pottery work, cow dung might do. And if there's a shortage of animal hair for weaving, wool, string or even nylon tights and metal shavings are perfectly acceptable.

The birds that consistently choose the strangest nesting material, however, are the corvids: crows, magpies, jays and the like. Most are omnivorous, meaning they will have a go at eating most things, which makes them perfectly adapted for urban life with its endless supply of items to satisfy both hunger and their insatiable curiosity. They particularly love shiny things, and all types of eye-catching objects have been found in their nests, from rings and watches to aluminum foil. In Tokyo, though, where crows have really taken to urban life, some have replaced their normal nesting material – large sticks – with shiny coat hangers, which they scavenge from rubbish bags. They have even perfected a way of carrying them in flight. There's a big problem for humans though: when the crows choose to nest on electricity pylons and drop a hanger or two, there is one massive electrical short-circuit.

NAME	**common crow**, hashiboso-garasu
	Corvus corone
LOCATION	Tokyo, Japan
ABILITY	making use of urban rubbish, in particular coat hangers, as nest material

Acknowledgements

With grateful thanks to the following scientists and experts who gave their valuable time to advise and comment.

Dr Duur Aanen, University of Copenhagen, Denmark; **Hilary Aikman,** Department of Conservation, Wellington, New Zealand; **Professor Kellar Autumn,** Lewis & Clark College, Oregon, USA; **Dr Jason Baker,** National Marine Fisheries Service, Honolulu, USA; **Bat Conservation International,** Texas, USA; **Professor Ernest C Bernard,** University of Tennessee, Knoxville, USA; **Kat Bolstad,** Auckland University of Technology, New Zealand; **Dr Elizabeth Brainerd,** University of Massachusetts, Amherst, USA; **Dr Mark Brazil,** Rakuno Gakuen University, Hokkaido, Japan; **Professor Lincoln Brower,** Sweet Briar College, Virginia, USA; **Professor Malcolm Burrows,** Department of Zoology, University of Cambridge, UK; **Dr Eliot Bush,** University of Chicago, Illinois, USA; **Dr Peter Buston,** National Center for Ecological Analysis and Synthesis, University of Santa Barbara, California, USA; **Dr John A Byers,** University of Idaho, Moscow, USA (author of *Built for Speed*); **Dr John A Byers,** Western Cotton Research Laboratory, United States Department of Agriculture – Agricultural Research Service, Arizona, USA; **Dr Tom Cade,** The Peregrine Fund, Boise, Idaho, USA; **Dr Janine Caira,** University of Connecticut, Storrs, USA; **Dr S Craig Cary,** Center for Marine Genomics, University of Delaware, USA; **Rogan Colbourne,** Department of Conservation, Wellington, New Zealand; **Professor William E Conner,** Wake Forest University, Winston-Salem, North Carolina, USA; **Dr Iain Couzin,** University of Oxford, UK; **Dr David Croft,** Arid Zone Field Station, University of New South Wales, Fowlers Gap, Australia; **Dr Alistair J Cullum,** Creighton University, Omaha, Nebraska, USA; **Dr John W Daly,** Scientist Emeritus, National Institute of Health, Bethesda, Maryland, USA; **Professor Frans B M de Waal,** Living Links Center, Emory University, Atlanta, Georgia 30322, USA (author of *Bonobo: The Forgotten Ape)*; **Dr W Richard J Dean,** Percy FitzPatrick Institute of African Ornithology, University of Cape Town, South Africa; **Dr Mark W Denny,** Hopkins Marine Station, Stanford University, California, USA; **Dr Andrew Derocher,** Edmonton, University of Alberta, Canada; **Professor Christopher R Dickman,** Institute of Wildlife Research and School of Biological Sciences, University of Sydney, New South Wales, Australia; **Dr Steve Diver,** University of Arkansas, Fayetteville, USA; **Professor Johan T du Toit,** Director, Mammal Research Institute, University of Pretoria, South Africa; **Professor Tom Eisner,** Section of Neurobiology and Behavior, Cornell University, USA; **Dr Mark Erdmann,** Senior advisor, Conservation International's Indonesia Marine Program; **Professor Frank E Fish,** West Chester University, USA; **Professor Charles Fisher,** The Pennsylvania State University, USA; **Dr Diana Fisher,** School of Botany and Zoology, Australian National University, Canberra, Australia; **Dr Matthias Foellmer,** St Mary's University, Halifax, Nova Scotia, Canada; **Dr Scott C France,** University of Louisiana, Lafayette, USA; **Dr Laurence Frank,** Museum of Vertebrate Zoology, University of California, Berkeley, USA; **Dr Douglas S Fudge,** University of Guelph, Ontario, Canada; **Dr Lisa Ganser,** University of Miami, Florida, USA; **Dr Randy Gaugler,** Rutgers University, New Jersey, USA; **Professor Ray Gibson,** John Moores University, Liverpool, UK; **Dr Cole Gilbert,** Department of Entomology, Cornell University, USA; **Dr Matthew R Gilligan,** Savannah State University, Georgia, USA; **Dr Ross L Goldingay,** Southern Cross University, Lismore, New South Wales, Australia; **Professor Gordon C Grigg,** University of Queensland, Brisbane, Australia; **Dr Paul D Haemig,** Umeå University, Sweden; **Professor Bill Hansson,** Department of Crop Science, Swedish University of Agricultural Sciences, Alnarp, Sweden; **Alice B Harper,** Aptos, California, USA; **Professor Peter Harrison,** Southern Cross University, New South Wales, Australia; **Dr S Blair Hedges,** Pennsylvania State University, USA; **Dr Wilbert Hetterscheid,** Curator, Botanical Gardens, Wageningen University, The Netherlands; **Dr A Rus Hoelzel,** University of Durham, UK; **Dr Carl D Hopkins,** Cornell University, Ithaca, New York, USA; **Dr David J Horne,** Queen Mary, University of London, UK; **Dr Ludwig Huber,** University of Vienna, Austria; **Dr Michael Huffman,** Kyoto University, Primate Research Unit, Japan; **Professor George Hughes,** University of Bristol, UK; **Dr Marina Hurley,** *Writing Clear Science*, Richmond South, Victoria, Australia; **Claudia Ihl,** University of Alaska, Institute of Arctic Biology, Fairbanks, Alaska, USA; **Paul Jansen,** Department of Conservation, Wellington, New Zealand; **Professor Jennifer U M Jarvis,** Zoology Department, University of Cape Town, South Africa; **Dr Judy Jernstedt,** University of California, Davis, USA; **Dr Reinhard Jetter,** University of British Columbia, Vancouver, Canada; **Professor Dale W Johnson,**

University of Nevada, Reno, USA; **Dr Darryl N Jones,** University of Queensland, Brisbane, Australia; **Dr Peter J Jones,** School of Biology, University of Edinburgh, UK; **Dr Stephen M Kajiura,** FAU Elasmobranch Research Laboratory Biological Sciences, Florida Atlantic University, USA; **Professor Ilan Karplus,** Aquaculture Research Unit, Ministry of Agriculture, Bet Dagan, Israel; **Professor Masashi Kawasaki,** University of Virginia, Charlottesville, USA; **Dr Rob Kay,** Laboratory of Molecular Biology, Medical Research Council, Cambridge, UK; **Professor Laurent Keller,** Department of Ecology and Evolution, University of Lausanne, Switzerland; **Professor Keith Kendrick,** Gresham Professor of Physic, Laboratory of Cognitive and Behavioural Neuroscience, The Babraham Institute, Cambridge, UK; **Dr Ian Kitching,** The Natural History Museum, London, UK; **Cor Kwant,** Amsterdam, The Netherlands; **Dr Jack R Layne Jr,** Slippery Rock University, Pennsylvania, USA; **Jonathan Leeming** www.scorpions.co.za; **Ashley Leiman,** The Orangutan Foundation, London; **Professor Douglas Levey,** University of Florida, Gainesville, USA; **A Jasmyn J Lynch,** University of Queensland, Gatton, Australia; **Dr Andrew L Mac,** Wildlife Conservation Society, Goroka, Papua New Guinea; **Dr Todd J McWhorter,** College of Agricultural & Life Sciences, University of Wisconsin, Madison, USA; **Dr Christopher D Marshall,** Department of Marine Biology, Texas A&M University, Galveston, Texas, USA; **Professor Justin Marshall,** Sensory Ecology Laboratory, Vision Touch and Hearing Research Centre, University of Queensland, Brisbane, Australia; **Chris Mattison,** Sheffield, UK; **Dr Mette Mauritzen,** Institute of Marine Research, Bergen, Norway; **Don Merton,** Department of Conservation, Wellington, New Zealand; **Dr Jay Meyers,** Northern Arizona University, Flagstaff, USA; **Dr Geoff Monteith,** Queensland Museum, Brisbane, Australia; **Dr John Morrissey,** Hofstra University Marine Laboratory, New York, USA; **Dr Ulrich G Mueller,** University of Texas, Austin, USA; **Dr Phil Myers,** Museum of Zoology, University of Michigan, Ann Arbor, USA; **Dr Mark Norman,** Museum Victoria, Melbourne, Australia; **Tim Osborne,** Kori Bustard Farming, Outjo, Namibia; **Peter Parks,** Image Quest Marine, Witney, Oxfordshire, UK; **Dr Julian C Partridge,** University of Bristol, UK; **Professor Jakob Parzefall,** Zoologica Institute and Zoological Museum, University of Hamburg, Germany; **Dr Irene Pepperberg,** Brandeis University, Massachusetts, USA; **Professor Eric R Pianka,** The University of Texas, Austin, USA; **Professor Theodore W Pietsch,** University of Washington, Seattle, USA; **Robin Prytherch,** Bristol, UK; **Gordon Ramel,** the Earthlife Web; **Dr Simon M Reader,** Utrecht University, The Netherlands; **Ian Redmond,** Bristol, UK; **Dr Eileen C Rees,** Wildfowl & Wetlands Trust, Martin Mere, Lancashire, UK; **Dr Barry A Rice,** University of California, Davis, USA/International Carnivorous Plant Society; **Dr Klaus Riede,** Zoological Research Institute and Museum Alexander Koenig (ZFMK), Bonn, Germany; **Dr Stephen Rossiter,** Queen Mary College, University of London, UK; **Royal Botanic Garden Edinburgh,** UK; **Dr Roy T Sawyer,** Biopharm Ltd, Wales, UK; **Dr John S Scheibe,** Southeast Missouri State University, Cape Girardeau, USA; **Dr Scott L Schliebe,** Marine Mammals Management, US Fish and Wildlife Service, Anchorage, Alaska, USA; **Jason C Seitz,** Florida Program for Shark Research, Florida Museum of Natural History, University of Florida, Gainesville, USA; **Professor Lynne Selwood,** University of Melbourne, Australia; **Dr Jamie Seymour,** James Cook University, Cairns, Queensland, Australia; **Professor Craig Sharp,** Brunel University, Middlesex, UK; **Colin Shawyer,** Wheathampstead, Hertfordshire, UK; **Professor Rick Shine,** University of Sydney, New South Wales, Australia; **Dr Stephen C Sillett,** Humboldt State University, Arcata, California, USA; **Dr Colin Simpfendorfer,** Center for Shark Research, Mote Marine Laboratory, Florida, USA; **Dr Jack T Sites Jr,** Brigham Young University, Provo, Utah, USA; **Nigel Sitwell,** Galapagos Conservation Trust, London, UK; **Dr Mike Siva-Jothy,** University of Sheffield, UK; **Dr David G Smith,** National Museum of Natural History, Smithsonian Institution, Washington DC, USA; **Dr Peter Speare,** Australian Institute of Marine Science, Townsville, Queensland, Australia; **Dr Brian Spooner,** Royal Botanic Gardens Kew, Richmond, Surrey, UK; **Dr Adam P Summers,** University of California, Irvine, USA; **Professor Sidney L Tamm,** Biology Department, Boston University, Boston, Massachusetts, USA; **Dr Andrew Taylor,** Wildlife Unit, Veterinary Sciences, University of Pretoria, South Africa; **Dr Robert J Thomas,** University of Cardiff, UK; **Dr Richard Thorington,** National Museum of Natural History, Smithsonian Institution, Washington, DC, USA; **Dr Michael Tyler,** University of Adelaide, South Australia; **Dr J Albert C Uy,** Syracuse University, USA; **Dr Richard Vari,** National Museum of Natural History, Smithsonian Institution, Washington DC, USA; **Dr Peter Vukusic,** Exeter University, Devon, UK; **H J Walker Jr,** Scripps Institution of Oceanography, University of California, San Diego, USA; **Dr Simon J Ward,** University of Melbourne, Parkville, Victoria, Australia; **William Watson,** NOAA Southwest Fisheries Science Center, La Jolla, California, USA; **Dr Grahame Webb,** Wildlife Management International, Sanderson, Northern Territory, Australia/Chairman IUCN-SSC Crocodile Specialist Group; **Dr Alexander Weir,** Behavioural Ecology Research Group, University of Oxford, UK; **Dr Barbara Wienecke,** Australian Antarctic Division, Tasmania, Australia; **Professor Oystein Wiig,** University of Oslo, Norway; **Dr Alex Wilson,** Center for Insect Science, University of Arizona, Tucson, Arizona, USA; **Professor Peter Wirtz,** Portugal; **Dr Jeffrey J Wood,** Royal Botanic Gardens, Kew, UK; **Dr William F Wood,** Humboldt State University, California, USA; **Dr Jennifer L Wortham,** University of Tampa, Florida, USA.

And a very special thank you to **Helen Brocklehurst** and **Rachel Ashton** for their invaluable advice, support, enthusiasm and encouragement from beginning to end.

Index